The Tao of Prepping

Spera optimum sed

Praepara ad pessimum

Edward O'Toole

First Edition

Multi-Media
Publications Inc.

Oshawa, Ontario

The Tao of Prepping
by Edward O'Toole

Managing Editor: Kevin Aguanno
Typesetting: Carolyn Prior
Cover Design: Carolyn Prior
eBook Conversion: Carolyn Prior

Published by:
Multi-Media Publications Inc.
Oshawa, ON

http://www.mmpubs.com/

www.edwardotoole.com

Paperback   ISBN-13: 978-1-55489-166-5

Published in Canada. Printed simultaneously in the United States of America, Australia and the United Kingdom.

CIP data available from the publisher.

Table of Contents

Dedication

For Babes (my Dark Age trophy wife), Bam-Bam, Mangle, Lynx, Babka, Weasel-Head, and the rest of my family.

After all, family is what it's all about.... Blood is blood.

"Nothing happens unexpectedly, everything has an indication, we just have to observe the connections."

—Zsolt Boszormeny, Head of RSOE EDIS, Emergency and Disaster Information Service

"Train yourself to avoid misfortunes by anticipating them in advance"

—Brian Browne Walker, Ts'ui, I Ching

Books by Edward O'Toole:

Sophia Bestiae

Grimoire Bestiae

Carpathian Ghost Hunter

Clavis

Windblown

Zen Gnosis

Also by Edward O'Toole and Eris-X:

Bestian Tarot

Science fiction writer Edward O'Toole... lives off the land in Slovakia as he believes it will give him a better chance of survival.

—Daily Mail

The king of the preppers was Edward... Edward's bug-out spot was in Slovakia on the edge of a game-filled forest.

—Radio Times

Foreword

Back in September 2012, *National Geographic* aired *"Preppers UK: Surviving Armageddon"*; one of those featured on the show was Edward O'Toole.

To date, he has been a regular visitor and contributor to P2S forum. He brings with him his unique insight into living "the life" at his retreat and, by virtue of doing so, reminds us that people can still survive, and indeed thrive, using the skills that many of us have unfortunately forgotten, or have never been privy to learning.

Edward talks of realising our sixth sense and it matters little if your forest is brick and concrete as opposed to Beech, Oak or Birch. You can still become tuned into your environment if you remove your blinkers.

Whilst in the UK the majority of us are living within each others' pockets, we are blessed with an abundant variety of green open spaces. Admittedly, some of those spaces are relatively small but they still provide us with an environment where we can practise many skills.

Many people are of the opinion that nothing bad will ever happen to them. But the ugly truth is that a disaster is always looming, waiting to pounce on the ill-prepared. For example:

December 2010 Northern Ireland - Water shortage.

A sudden thaw after Arctic conditions burst thousands of pipes and resulted in reservoirs running dry. This resulted in approximately 40,000 homes being left without running water. Supermarkets and shops were swamped with customers trying to purchase bottled water. Eventually, 17 distribution centres were set up, and some saw queues of 400 desperate people wanting drinking water. Doctors warned of a Public Health emergency.

That nightmare ran for seven days.

Yet, with a little knowledge and preparation, people could have ridden out the storm and provided for themselves.

Knowledge weighs nothing and, generally speaking, your knowledge can't be lost or stolen, and the *Tao of Prepping* really does enforce that notion.

Consumerism is the curse of modern life and preparedness has not escaped that curse. Preparedness and self-reliance should be primarily skill-based and never just "kit" based and, again, Edward really does strive to get that point across.

There are perhaps thousands of books available to read on survival and self-reliance and many just cover "beans, bullets and band aids". *The Tao of Prepping* definitely adds something that many miss and should be an essential read for all those that have chosen to break their own trail in preparedness.

Allan Beecher, AKA Dark Vengeance, the owner/ founder of P2S. an online (and offline) survival and self-reliance community for like-minded people. http://www.p2s-prepared2survive.co.uk/

August 2013

Introduction

"Every day when one's body and mind are at peace, one should meditate upon being ripped apart by arrows, rifles, spears and swords, being carried away by surging waves, being thrown into the midst of a great fire, being struck by lightning, being shaken to death by a great earthquake, falling from thousand-foot cliffs, dying of disease ..."

—Ghost Dog (paraphrasing Yamamoto Tsunetomo, Hagakure)

I stood in my garden shortly before dusk. The sky was still blue with the occasional cloud dotted just above the horizon, burning some orangey-pink. Beyond the deer fence, the hillside had recently been mown and harvested, which had encouraged mice back into the house but it also meant that it was now easier to walk up the hill to the deep deciduous forest beyond.

A few plots of land over, an old man was mowing with a scythe, cutting his tall grass to feed his livestock: a couple of goats and some rabbits kept in vertically stacked hutches. Dogs barked somewhere in the village, defending their territories from their chains. Tall ox-eye daisies stood in clumps like little islands, hiding the deer as they began to come out to graze. Crickets and grasshoppers chirped because of the continuing heat, and cicadas slowly began to emerge in the trees for their nocturnal chorus.

All about were a myriad of greens; each of the tree types bearing its own distinct greenness. At ground level, the grass, the clover, the plantain, the nettles, the hemlock, the parsley, the mint, all a different shade of green. Blue above, green below, green all about, with the occasional bright flash of colour from a late summer flower, or from a startled cloud as the sun gave up its daily crawl. This all made me think.

I'd often questioned myself as to why I'm here in this remote corner of Europe, why I left the busy modern world, why I try to raise a family out in the bush. I often ask myself "Who am I?" Sometimes, I forget. I get distracted as I see the purple heads of the dock flower, or the yellow of the camomile or the buttercup, or as I see the blackberries in fruit, replacing the now withered raspberries at the edge of my garden, or when I see the nuts bowing the delicate hazel, or the purple and yellow plums pulling down heavily on their trees, bending the boughs.

I often ask myself "Who am I and why am I here? Why did I give up the modern world? Why didn't I stay in a big city surrounded by technology, fast cars, fast people?" When I walk my little Jack

Russell on the abandoned road that runs up into the
Carpathian foothills and look down on the valley in
which my house, and the ancient Ruthenian village,
is situated, I understand why.

Over the years, I've encountered many others who
find themselves thinking these very same thoughts
but who haven't quite yet made that giant leap into
nowhere; who haven't quite completely turned their
backs on the modern world for whatever reason:
family, mortgage, job, etc.

This book is for those who feel that there is
something missing in how they live their lives. It's
for those who feel that call of nature, to be at one
with it. It's for those who understand that our fast-
paced, gimme-gimme modern life can end in a flash
and leave us back at square one and that, without
a proper understanding of the world and a decent
skill-set, we could find ourselves in extremely dire
circumstances.

There are many different reasons why people get
into prepping and what they're prepping for. Some
believe the end is nigh, others believe in fantastic
situations such as a zombie apocalypse or asteroid
devastation, or a pole shift, and there are others who
worry that they might lose their job and not have
enough food to feed their family. There are others
who believe that modern civilization is at an end,
whether because of peak oil or merely just because
of bad economic play by world powers, and that the
civilized nations will see riots and droughts and
starvation on an epic scale and who want to protect
their family from this.

"In order to change an existing paradigm you do not struggle to try and change the problematic model. You create a new model and make the old one obsolete."

—Buckminster Fuller

Many get into prepping from the old survivalist school, many are ex-soldiers, many are already homesteaders, or want to be homesteaders, and many are just everyday people – office workers, factory workers, the unemployed - who look about themselves and see that there is something fundamentally missing or wrong with being glued to a screen or monitor day after day.

These people, those who are only just beginning their journey, are often overwhelmed by the more experienced prepper, those with full larders or armouries or bunkers or small holdings. But out of all the books and films and TV series and forums and blogs and magazines that I've encountered to do with prepping, I've never once seen or heard of anyone questioning the philosophical or spiritual aspect of it. If we reduce bushcraft or prepping or homesteading to a purely materialist activity then we are little better than those who just follow a football club or *X Factor*.

Our greatest asset is the record of primitive and tribal societies, and how they functioned, how they survived. We can learn from them and apply those lessons to the modern world. Mix primitive survival techniques with modern technology; but we must remember that a fundamental aspect of all human history was the spiritual side, a spiritual connection to nature, to the forest, to the trees that we use to build, to burn, to the game we hunt, the animals we raise for food. Each has its own soul and it's essential that we learn to reconnect to this.

"Success depends upon previous preparation, and without such preparation there is sure to be failure."

—Confucius

Prepping should not be just about buying the most expensive equipment. In fact that is the most illogical thing to do. If we are aiming to survive some major cataclysmic event, we need to be more in-tune with our environment, and we cannot be in-tune with our environment if we need massive amounts of resources just to produce basic items.   We need to become far more resourceful, as our ancestors, as our grandparents were. We need to be more aware of what's around us. We need to know how to reuse things, how to use things in diverse ways for multiple uses.

We need to tear ourselves away from the commercial aspect that is rammed down our throats. We have become a disposable society but, in reality, we don't dispose of anything, we just hide it, we dump it, and it becomes a future generation's problem. We use resources to create something which we don't really need, or we already have existing functioning versions of, and these resources are not renewable, or not in any time frame we can conceive of.

It is my aim to introduce some of these simple thoughts back into the prepping, the bushcraft, the homesteading community.

I don't intend on instructing how to make jam or an EMP-proof generator, as there are others far more knowledgeable on this, and other areas, than me in this respect. I don't intend to give equipment reviews for the latest *tacticool* gear because, for many, these items are far too specialized or far too expensive, and this can deter people from even beginning to prep.

Just like our ancestors, we need the bare minimal equipment, we need to know what we need and how to look after it, and the skills to use it; these things I will try to explain. A bit like bushcrafting on a budget but not for purely economic reasons, instead because it should become a necessity to think in that manner, not to waste. To remove lust and jealousy and desire from our thinking. It's far too easy to look at someone who has been doing prepping or survivalism for decades and feel inner anger that we don't have their micro-lite tent or their hand-forged hunting knife or their completely waterproof five-season boots or their home jarring equipment. But this is just an illusion. None of these things are truly necessary.

First and foremost, we must deal with our inner thinking and our own way of being and our own reasons for being. We must become content in ourselves, with ourselves and with what we have at our disposal. If we are lucky enough to have the money to spend on bucketfuls of equipment then we should refrain from doing so until we understand, absolutely, the basics. It's like passing the driving test and immediately getting an all-electronic luxury car but not understanding why such gadgets as cruise control or nitrous oxide injection improve on the basic, standard, engine, steering wheel, driver's seat and four-wheels model.

I can now hear a sad dirge from a radio playing somewhere in the village. It's some local version of a bagpipe and it fills the air, almost weeping for the sun's setting. Although the environment here is deciduous, there are still a few coniferous trees proudly jutting skywards, and they appear to mark the boundary of the music itself.

I've spent the last 15 years living in a remote part of Eastern Slovakia, among the *Rusyn* (Ruthenian) people. I've seen the effect that globalization has had on the region, and the subsequent rapid decline in use of traditional skills. I count myself very lucky that I arrived before the strimmmer and mower replaced the scythe, the supermarket replaced the pig and potato patch, mains gas replaced the wood burning pec, the tractor replaced the horse and plough, and the rotivator replaced old *Babkas* in traditional dress tending their fields.

I've tried to learn how things were done, and we've raised our children half in the modern, technological world and half in the ancient but still extant. Compared to the born-and-bred villagers, I'm an absolute amateur and, on many occasions, I've felt embarrassed that I don't know how to do something *in my bones* as they seem to. Expertise in self-reliance and self-sufficiency appear to be genetically inherited out here.

I live in one of the most beautiful places on Earth, in the Carpathian Mountain range. Yes, there are things I miss from the West but when I wake and am confronted by a Tolkienesque landscape teeming with beasts, birds, insects, reptiles, amphibians, butterflies, forest and wildflowers, I remember why I'm here.

I wish the world could see and understand just how important this region is for Man's survival; there are so many things to learn from its ageless wisdom of both living with and managing Nature, yet there seems so little time left.

Wisdom comes from understanding experiential knowledge. The more we experience, the more we know, the more we understand, the wiser we become.

While this book may be in theoretical form, I can only hope that it encourages the reader to experience for themselves an alternative, healthier and much more logical lifestyle than the one currently accepted as the norm.

Self-reliance empowers the weak, it allows the poor the dignity to feed and clothe themselves and their family without having to beg from the State, and it provides an almost infinite testing ground for the strong to prove their own mettle.

The future begins with the present.

Edward O'Toole

Svidník, Slovakia, 2013

Prepping – what it is and why you should be doing it

I hear hurricanes ablowing.
I know the end is coming soon.
I fear rivers over flowing.
I hear the voice of rage and ruin

—Bad Moon Rising, Creedence Clearwater
Revival

We live, at the beginning of the 21st Century, in a world filled with seemingly magical technology. We can fly around the world, we can chat face-to-face with anyone in the world in real-time, we can heat our homes and cook our meals at the touch of a button and without the use of flame. We work in offices and we're skilled in redistributing paper and numbers, or at making pictures and letters appear on electronic screens; or, we work in factories where we assemble parts or put them in boxes.

We spend our free time staring at one electronic box or another, and then discuss what we have seen with others.

We know that food comes pre-packaged from a supermarket and that we pay for it using a small plastic rectangle, which we refill – if we are lucky – by working in an office or factory.

If we don't work, we know that the Government will give us money so that we can go to the supermarket and buy pre-packaged food to feed our families.

We drink sweetened, carbonated water from plastic bottles and we spend much of our time talking or tapping messages into a little plastic box permanently held at our ears.

We live in homes owned by someone else – either we rent from a landlord or we take immense loans from banks for an unnecessarily large McMansion, and then spend the rest of our lives trying to pay them back. We borrow money so that we can have the latest car or television because the magic box in our living rooms told us we need them, even though they will be made deliberately obsolete within a few years and then we'll have to repeat the entire process again, keeping us permanently in debt.

Our children have been raised on quasi-foodstuffs filled with toxins but we only either buy from big brand names or supermarket-own. The old fear the young, the young respect no-one and everyone hates immigrants. And the land has been fenced off and divided between a few individuals or corporations who use it to experiment with genetically modified crops which we are told are healthy, but the mass extinction of wildlife – especially the honey bees, which are solely responsible for pollinating one quarter of the world's plant-life – suggests otherwise.

It has got to the stage where a growing number of individuals wish to turn their backs on such an artificial and claustrophobic society, and return to a healthier more traditional one. Some, known as preppers, bushcrafters, homesteaders or survivalists, prepare for a time when society will fail so that they can start again.

There are scientifically plausible scenarios which could see the end of our civilization, events which would plunge us back into a Dark Age of sorts – solar flares, global economic meltdown, climate change, war. But the *Tao of Prepping* isn't about carrying on as is and hoping that things will change dramatically at some point in the future. This book is about changing now, at an individual level.

A few generations back it was common for people to put something aside for a rainy day – to stock up on extra food for winter, to hide some cash in the mattress, and to save anything which could be reused, such as shoelaces and nails. Fast forward to the 21st Century, a world of electronic banking, hypermarkets stocked with global produce, HD TVs, social welfare, universally available medical care, credit and mortgages; a world where many of us can't even make it to the next pay day without borrowing money, a gimme-gimme world of instant appeasement where dinner comes in a plastic wrap and is paid for with a plastic card.

Let's just imagine for a moment what would happen if something, some catastrophic event, threw a spanner into the precisely interconnected cogs which keep this modern, globalised, civilization running. There are a few possible scenarios which could really hit us hard and which, surprisingly, we've actually been warned about by the powers that be: being slammed by a meteor or rogue planet (just ask the dinosaurs about that one); an immense solar flare and CME frying the electrical grid and showering us with falling, nuclear-powered satellites; extreme weather fluctuations (drought, flood, drought, flood, mini Ice Age); nuclear disaster; civil unrest; the end of oil, and so on.

"They went into stores to get food to stay alive. Looting isn't the right word. I call it survival."

—Russel Honore

To give yourself a better idea of what to expect in such a situation, watch video footage from Hurricane Katrina – because the population of New Orleans was largely unprepared, they panicked. Supermarket shelves rapidly emptied and people began to fight over the remaining limited resources. Tap water became undrinkable because it was infected with sewerage. Law and order went out the window and, for a short time, it became a dog-eat-dog world. If you think this couldn't happen again, or that it couldn't happen where you live, think again.

No matter how advanced we think we are, we're always just one disaster away from barbarity.

However, not all of us are in a position to build a bunker or move to some theoretically safer exotic location – job, school, family, and mortgage mean we may just have to work with what we've got. A lack of disposable income is a hurdle, not a dead end – there are things that everyone can do to give themselves and their families a bit of a head start on those who don't prepare, and the longer you can ensure your survival, the more chance you and your family have of surviving in the long term.

Many preppers will recommend that you stock up on vast quantities of food. If you can't afford to splash out in your favourite supermarket then just buy a couple of extra items each time you go shopping – look for tinned foods with long expiry dates, dried food, dehydrated food, chocolate, anything that will last. If you keep doing this regularly you'll soon find you have quite a bit of food in reserve – just remember to use it before it goes bad, rotating and replacing it with newer goods. Make sure you store it in a way that rodents and insects can't get to it, and don't tell your neighbours. If disaster does strike you *really* don't want to be known as the only local food source.

Don't plan on living off rabbits and squirrels: for one thing, everyone else will have the same idea and, for another, you'll die from malnutrition as they have very little fat content (which you need to digest the protein from the meat).

You'll also need fuel for cooking and heating. Unless you happen to have a huge tank of butane in your garden, or a coal seam, then you'll need to find a local, replenishable fuel source. That means wood. Lots and lots of wood. Pine is useless for everything but Scandinavian pre-packed furniture, so look for broad leaf trees like beech and oak.

Most importantly of all, though, you'll need skills.

There's an old survival axiom which states that the more you know, the less you need. Don't plan on getting and reading, or even worse carrying if you plan on bugging out, lots of books. Learn skills now. Enrol in a first aid course, learn welding, plumbing and carpentry, how to purify water, study what your body needs to survive. And then, and this is the most important piece of advice of all, go and practice.

Learn through experience.

There's a world of difference between what you see on TV or read in a book and how it works in a real life situation. Try spending a week without mod-cons, even take your family to the forest and practice your skills.

Don't rely on equipment. Learn how to improvise.

Practice, practice, practice.

Each time you make a mistake you'll become wiser, and it's far better to discover your faults while civilization is still up and running than leaving it all until the last minute when the SHTF. Because then it will be too late.

As the Romans would have said:

Spera optimum sed, praepara ad pessimum
– hope for the best but prepare for the worst.

As a prepper, your future is literally in your hands.

The Journey

"Thinking about things previously and then handling them lightly when the time comes is what this is all about"

—Yamamoto Tsunetomo, Hagakure

Some journeys are physical, moving yourself from Point A to Point B. Some journeys are mental or spiritual, moving yourself from an old thought or mindset to a new one.

This evening, I turned my car off the main road and onto the small winding one which leads to my village. There is a precise point, several hundred yards before this turning, which affects me emotionally each time I reach it, regardless of the time of day or the season. In all climates it's awe-inspiring.

The last of the monotonous, straight-rowed villages, with houses clinging uniformly to the roadside, slips into the distance behind me, I go over a series of incredibly deep potholes and then I see the valley open up on my left. The trees are thickly-packed and apparently never-ending, the shallow river winds its way around a floodplain and disappears into the tree-line, where it continues to hug the road until I reach my village. There are twists and curves in the road so I have to drive slowly, meaning I take in more of my surroundings than if I was travelling at speed. At night, large beasts dart across the road, their eyes reflecting my headlights, and I often have to brake sharply to avoid colliding with an immense deer or boar.

In the spring, this journey is filled with the smell of wild garlic, in summer dense foliage, in autumn reds and yellows interspersed with the odd evergreen, and in winter everywhere and everything is white.

This five mile stretch of nowhere road, from the point of awe to the Cyrillic and Latin road-signs which denote entry into my village, is a journey of metamorphosis in its own right. I leave behind the urban mindset and smart clothes at the point where the valley begins and, by the time I've reached my village, I'm longing to put on a pair of old combats and go chop some wood, or take the dog up the hill into the forest in search of berries or mushrooms, or just to reconnect to the power of the wild.

"No one is more of a slave than he who thinks himself free without being so."

—Johann Wolfgang von Goethe

In reality, the entire transformation happens inside my own mind. The logical would say it is all just fantasy, but I would have to disagree. It's all about opening yourself up and, for however brief a moment, putting away your everyday self and allowing yourself to feel free. Once that freedom of thought has been reached, the next step is to become aware of what's around you, to soak it up and become part of it. To live it, if but for the briefest of time.

It's all about transformation, and the journey towards that. Only the most wilful of people can decide to completely change their lives and do so from one moment to the next. Usually, we dip our toes in the water many times before deciding that we'd like to swim. Prepping, bushcraft and homesteading are like that. While we'd all like to give up our day jobs and get paid to go off into the wilderness with just a camera for company, it's extremely unlikely that will happen. Many of us would like to sell our terrace home, if we even own it, and move to a remote cottage with kitchen garden and acreage, and live off the land; simple economics dictates otherwise. But we can begin that journey, one toe-dip at a time.

What's important is that when you do something, no matter what it is, you do and think about only that, be completely into it and at one with it. If you decide to try your hand at jarring then mentally prepare for it, read up on it, do some research, prepare your foodstuffs and equipment, look forward to it and then, when you actually begin the activity itself, imagine that that is all you do. Picture yourself in your own homestead doing that very same activity. Imagine that your life depended on it for future food so don't do it half-heartedly or give up halfway through.

The same goes for if you decide to spend the night in the woods under a tarpaulin. Yes, you will get cold; yes, you will get constantly harassed by mosquitoes and gnats; yes, the ground will feel uncomfortable under your back, but be completely with that situation. Imagine that you can't just say "sod it", pack your stuff and drive home to a nice warm bed, a mug of cocoa and a late night rerun of some cookery programme. Imagine that there is no going back. Force yourself to face the elements. The sense of achievement you will feel when you awake the next morning, damp with dew and with a crick in your neck is thousands of times better than the sense of guilt and shame you'll feel if you'd called it quits and gone home.

I'm not saying you should push yourself to the limits but you should always push yourself a little harder than you thought you could manage. And, each time you push yourself, you're one step closer to the goal of self-reliance, which is all about having the confidence to stand on your own two feet.

The modern world constantly tells us that waiting and learning are bad and that we should expect instant gratification. Picture your journey as that of an apprentice in the old days, who spent seven years doing the most menial of tasks for the master, thinking that they weren't learning anything, and then who had to do another seven years as a journeyman.

Everything you do, and everywhere you go, teaches you something useful, but only if you are completely focused on it.

Making mistakes can be far more beneficial than doing things perfectly each time you try them. Experience is the greatest teacher.

Don't be put off by know-it-alls or those who criticize without being constructive. Learn from those with more experience and knowledge but don't just copy; try to do things on your own and at your own pace. If you feel something isn't for you then don't do it.

Every journey is ultimately undertaken alone, even when we're lucky that others join us for part of it. And, as you make your journey to self-awareness and self-reliance, return the favour and help others who are just starting out. Knowledge should always be shared, never squandered or selfishly kept hidden away.

Tao of Prepping

Where am I?

"I live in my own little world. But it's okay, they know me here."

—Lauren Myracle

"And God said, Behold, I have given you every herb bearing seed, which is upon the face of all the earth, and every tree, in the which is the fruit of a tree yielding seed; to you it shall be for meat."

—Genesis 1:29, KJV

I put on a shirt because the mosquitoes had begun to bite and the bats hadn't yet taken to the wing and left the wooden storehouse at the edge of my land. The solar-powered LED lights which encircle my garden, or sit disguised as rocks in the flower bed, had come on and added a weak glow, but they weren't really needed yet.

They make me think of so many useless items
we acquire which we do not need, which are not
necessary and fulfil only the function of temporary
amusement, or for paying the advertising company
which promoted them, or the production company
which manufactured them, or the design team which
designed them. But for us, we who worked and saved
our money, and instead of spending that precious
money on useful things such as food for our family,
or goods which might last for the future and help
us to grow, we spent our money on these things,
gimmicks and gadgets which last but a short time
before they break or we tire of them, or we're told
they're outdated and we shove them in a cupboard
and forget about them. And, how quickly we forget
how we lost the money and the goods, when both
could have been better used somewhere, and on
something, else.

Where am I?

I have great respect for those who've taken the time
and dedication to first learn the skills needed to
survive and help their families survive, and then go
on to write books about it, or to create educational
programmes about it, to help others learn also, but
I've always had this major problem that often with
the majority of the texts, the activities described,
and the fauna and flora listed therein, bear little
semblance to those necessary around me. While
I'm sure it's very useful to know what to do in the
subarctic tundra, should my plane crash there, or on
a tropical island, if I ever find myself marooned, it is
also highly unlikely that I'll ever need such skills or
need to know what types of animals or birds or fish
to eat there, which plants poison and which plants
heal.

There is an old Zen *koan* about a tea cup and the metaphor is about knowledge, or planned activities. That until the tea cup is emptied you cannot put any more tea in it. Similarly, if we fill our minds with the vast information available to us, for example from the Internet, we do not become more skilled or more knowledgeable, we just become more distilled. If we plan to do too many things, we end up doing none, or just a few poorly. Focus on doing one activity, or resolving one problem, and empty the tea cup, before taking on another and refilling it.

It is far better to ask yourself the question "Where am I?" and then focus on that, than to learn about the far reaches of the world unless you really intend to find yourself in those locations. While it is interesting to know about the life-cycle of freshwater dolphins in the Amazon, it is not very likely that these will become part of your diet on the River Dee or Thames.

The happiest people I've ever met are those who were born and raised in a village and never left. They lived simple lives and weren't exposed enough to the outside world to become confused and begin hating their lives and wishing that they were someone or somewhere else.

A Special Place

"There is a pleasure in the pathless woods,
There is a rapture on the lonely shore,
There is society, where none intrudes,
By the deep sea, and music in its roar:
I love not man the less, but Nature more."

—Lord Byron, Childe Harold's Pilgrimage

What I'd like for you to do now is to go to your favourite natural spot, whether physically if possible, or just mentally. Just take yourself there, separate yourself from external concerns. Be there and only there, and ask yourself "Where am I?"

Look about you, what plant life do you see? What trees? What birds do you hear, do you see? What animals? If there is water, do you see fish, do you see crayfish, crustaceans, water boatmen?

Smell the air. What can you smell?

We have five senses. Touch the bark of a tree. Stroke your fingers along it. Feel where it is dry, feel where it is gnarly, feel where it is mossy, feel its knots and holes. Be with the tree. If you can, take off your shoes. Feel the dirt or the grass or the leaves beneath your feet.

Listen. Listen to the wind. Listen to how the wind moves through the branches, the leaves. Turn your face to the wind and feel it brush against your skin. Feel if it contains the moisture of rain or if it's dry or if it presages frost.

Five senses.

When you are completely in tune with five senses to your surroundings, the sixth sense becomes apparent. When you truly know your location, you know when something isn't right, when something is there which shouldn't be, or something isn't there which should. That is the sixth sense. It's the knowledge and awareness of where you are.

As darkness slowly falls, and the clouds become as shadows of bluey-grey, and the tiniest pinpricks of stars begin to emerge in the deep, dark blue of the night above, moths circle around and, out there, beyond the deer fence, herds are moving. Roe deer, Red Deer, wild boar, entire troops of sows and piglets, wolves roam the forests, lynx hunt beneath the trees, Eurasian raccoons scamper along branches, beavers chew down saplings and block dried stream-beds, pine martens fight in my attic, owls, falcons, eagles, fox, badger... I'm surrounded by wildlife. Absolutely surrounded. Wild, wild game. Their presence is part of my children's lives.

A mere trip to the forest is never one of complete relaxation. While the forest is beautiful and enticing, it is also a place of risk, where the hunter hunts the hunted and the circle of life continues daily. An animal is born, another dies or is killed; an animal eats, another is eaten, and there are creatures out there in the forest which see the lone human as merely another part of the food chain, or a threat to defend against. But being part of that cycle is like stepping back thousands of years into a more primal existence, where Man truly was part of the cycle of nature, where looking for fungi in the detritus and humus of fallen leaves on the forest floor, or foraging for berries, was part and parcel of daily life, whilst keeping an eye and ear out at all times for four-legged danger with snarling, and sharp teeth, or huge curled tusks which, in a flash, could disembowel and end a hunter's life.

But the forest, even if it is just a copse of trees somewhere on a public heath, or even in a park, is a means of reconnecting, reconnecting between our modern, disjointed, confused selves with the more primal aspect of our character, one which has been buried, so deeply, by constant pressure from the media, from peers, from schools, from work, from financial stress.

For some, their special place to commune is not a forest, but an open, windswept moor, or a beach, or a mountain peak, or a fen filled with reeds and brackish water . It's not important where your special location is, in which you feel reconnected to the earth; what is important is that you find that place.

Before we begin our journey into the *Tao of Prepping*, we need a root, we need to find a place which we can call our primal home, where we feel at one with our surroundings.

While television channels such as *Discovery*, *National Geographic*, or *Viasat Explorer* encourage us to imagine exotic locations such as Alaska or the Congo or Siberia as being the only places fit for the true survivalist, this is not true. The true survivalist means only having a place where they can walk and think and be in tune with their primal selves – and be able to survive there. It is important to distance yourself from the stresses of modern life, if but for a brief instance, so we will begin by finding that place.

Think where you like to walk your dog, is there a place you often head to? Is there a place you go to pick up kindling? Is there a place you go to just sit and watch the view? Is there a special place which reminds you of happier, more innocent times, or a place where the aroma of flowers entices you? It could even be on the open water, on a boat, where you feel the waves lapping against the sides. I want you to take yourself to that place and explore it, truly explore it.

We are prepping with reality in mind. If something does happen, if there is a disaster, you're going to need to go somewhere pretty close to home. You're not going to be able to hop on a plane and travel half way around the world, or head out to the Australian Outback and live as an Aboriginal, not unless Alice Springs is in your neighbourhood.

Your best option is to know what is around you, and the best way to start that is by going out to it, spending time there, accustoming yourself to its little whims and fancies and faults.

To begin with, ignore the signs of humanity and habitation. Look for the majesty of nature in whatever form she appears, and attune yourself to that. I want you to hold onto that image, to those smells, to those sounds. Learn and be that location because it is from there that our journey begins.

Bug In or Bug Out?

"He that is far off shall die of the pestilence; and he that is near shall fall by the sword; and he that remaineth and is besieged shall die by the famine: thus will I accomplish my fury upon them"

—Ezekiel 6:12, KJV

"Remember the Alamo!"

—General Sam Houston

The term *prepper* often conjures up the image of obese red-neck paranoiacs hunkering down in their bunker basement, armed to the teeth and surrounded by buckets of food. This could be termed *Bugging In*. The term *survivalist* often conjures up the image of a middle-aged bloke wearing army surplus, living in a lean-to and scoffing down rabbits and road kill, in a copse of woods twenty feet from a main road. That could be termed *Bugging Out*. The reasons for choosing either option are extensive and depend heavily on the individual bugger and their location...

And both images are blatantly false.

In an ideal Apocalypse, we'd convert our semi-detached into a fortified, food-laden, heavily-armed harem and laugh heartily at the ignorant masses *out there*. At least until the food supply ran out. In practice, Bugging-In is akin to a fox going to ground and, when available external resources dwindle, the local populace is going to get a lot more brazen in their quest for their daily staples. Remember the Alamo? I'll bet Davy Crockett and Jim Bowie were kicking themselves when they realized they were completely surrounded and there was no chance left to Bug Out.

You have to know this for yourself. Really take some time thinking about it. Do you plan to stay in suburbia and compete for resources with the locals, or do you plan to get out of Dodge and run to the hills? There are pros and cons either way. If you're not used to roughing it in the bush, you're probably not going to last long – unless you start practising now, that is.

The ideal situation is Bugging Out to Bug In, e.g. having a remote retreat already set up where you can head to when the SHTF. And I mean really set up – you'll need accommodation, fresh water, food supply, latrines, renewable fuel source, defensible position, etc.

Most people prepare for the 72 hours scenario. This is where there's a natural disaster such as an earthquake, flood, or hurricane and you need to be self-reliant for a couple of days until the Nanny State can switch your water and electricity back on and you can go back to using your games console or watching amateur wannabe pop stars plagiarizing modern classics on TV.

For many preppers and survivalists this is the extent of their forecast, and many take great pleasure in researching and then buying the coolest gizmos necessary to get through it, and get through it well. But what happens if 72 hours turns into 72 weeks, or months even? Just how many tins and pre-packed dehydrated rations are you prepared to stash, or defend?

Prepare for the worst and hope for the best, set yourself the target of surviving the worst case scenario and anything less than that will seem like a walk in the park. For any situation lasting longer than a couple of weeks, you're going to need a well-stocked, well-prepared getaway location.

During the Blitz, Londoners helped one another and collectively sang songs in the Underground to keep spirits high; during Hurricane Katrina, the population of New Orleans robbed, raped and murdered each other for bottles of water – and that was after only a couple of days. Your guess is as good as mine but times have changed so I'm leaning away from the *Knees up Muvva Brown* sing-a-long with gangsters, fundamentalists and hoodies.

The ultimate aim of survival is to be completely self-sufficient and self-reliant. A community made up of such individuals is a Utopia. But in the modern, pre-

Apocalyptic world, money is Master. Everyone would like a house in the country with a kitchen garden but not everyone works in banks or in parliament. There are cheaper alternatives (free is nearly always good, *Remember you're a Womble!*) and it's worth remembering that in a really dire complete-breakdown-of-society situation, it is unlikely that every bit of farmland or forest will be as private as it currently is. Scope out suitable locations with a mind to taking up residence there should such needs arise. Obviously, if you buy or even just rent the land now you can set up your retreat however you please so when the sirens go off your only concern will be taking a walk and then putting the kettle on. If that is not an option, *recce* possible locales and work out what you'll need to make them viable for long-term habitation, and then work out where you'll get all the equipment you'll need to do so.

Whether you're planning on Bugging In at your current home or Bugging Out, just make sure you know what you'll need and make sure you either have such items at hand or at least have easy access to them in a potentially volatile environment.

> *"There are no secrets to success. It is the result of preparation, hard work, and learning from failure."*
>
> Colin Powell

Prior planning prevents poor performance – in this case, prior planning prevents you starving to death, being eaten by your neighbours or becoming their gimp, or freezing to death on some windswept barren moor whilst munching down on a bloated sheep carcass, just like they show on TV.

When it comes to choosing between urban and rural survival, it's the woods for me, hands down, every time. Unless you're already a pimp daddy with a well-armed crew and with your own fortified warehouse then leave the city behind. If you are an urbanite and do plan on staying put in the concrete jungle then start developing a support network of fellow preppers now.

There is only an estimated 3 days worth of food in the supply chain at any one time. That means if the trucks stop coming there'll be no food and if you're living in an area with a high population density you're going to quickly be surrounded by absolute chaos and pandemonium. When your water main gets cut off, and all the lights go out, you're on your own against an angry, hungry, confused and potentially violent population. If your plan was to suck water from puddles through a survival straw, or forage discarded produce from a market, then you're already dead.

There are only 3 days worth of food (actually much less when people start panic buying, and then looting) so you should ideally put yourself more than 3 days' walk away from the large population centres. After a week or so the population will have been reduced somewhat and will have settled into a brutal quasi-tribal existence so it will be a while yet before they start roaming further, in gangs, to forage and *womble*. By that time you should have made your Bug In retreat well fortified.

Just get out of the city.

However, if you are an urbanite, e.g. someone born and raised in a city, and you're not planning on Bugging In there, then start spending time in the bush now. Get used to it. If you've spent your entire life surrounded by mod-cons and 24-hour shops, supplying yourself and your family with their daily dietary requirements day in day out in a field or forest might not be as easy as you'd thought.

Location, location, location

"Man's heart away from nature becomes hard."

—Standing Bear

The Tao of Prepping doesn't deal with urban survival, it recommends that you get as far away from the city and as quickly as possible. As such, we're going to look at rural BO and rural BI.

In rural BO, you're basically going to last for as long as your food supply holds up + 5 days, and then you'll be too weak to hunt. If you really know what you're doing and have experience rabbiting and scrumping, you'll last a while longer. But not indefinitely. The roaming hunter-gatherer is a romantic ideal but it's just not feasible in modern, civilized countries. There aren't enough wild resources and there are too many people. It worked when we lived in small bands and moved camp every few months, allowing the local flora and fauna chance to recover for the next year. Once the supermarkets have been emptied, every wild animal and bird, every crop left in the field, every fruit in the trees will be harvested by the hungry masses. They simply will not understand that to have a deer or rabbit population the following year you can't kill and eat them all now.

Make foraging a supporting aspect of your plan but don't hinge on it or you will starve. The same goes for fishing, especially if we lose power as there will then follow umpteen industrial accidents which could pollute the waterways. If you live near the sea then yes, fishing will most likely provide your staple diet - unless there are oil spills - but not if you're inland. You really need to get your head around the idea of Bugging Out to Bug In – you need to choose a location where you can start your own homestead. The first few months of a long-term cataclysm will be chaotic and violent but gradually you'll have less competition and the number of hungry mouths will dwindle, enabling you to start really working on your family's future.

> *"For it is we who must pray for our daily bread, and if He grants it to us, it is only through our labour, our skill and preparation."*
>
> —Paracelsus

I've seen a few survivalists who've got half-way to
the right idea – they've chosen a remote parcel of
forest, with a stream. So far so good. However, the
ancient deciduous (broad-leaf) woodland of Britain
has virtually disappeared and has been replaced by
Forestry Commission coniferous (pine) plantations
– lots of Christmas trees evenly spaced in rows;
quick growing lumber for the timber industry. For
the survivalist, this is a dead zone. For firewood,
pine is awful as it produces little heat and gives off
acrid smoke; pine is useless for making bows; for
growing root vegetables the land is barren as fallen
pine needles make the soil too acidic and the native
undergrowth hasn't adapted to this environment,
the humus of which would give a more balanced soil.
The fact that there is no native undergrowth in the
pine plantations means nothing worth foraging, and
no little critters. If you're bugging out in a natural
pine zone (above 1200 metres for Scots Pine) then
the local flora and fauna will have evolved to provide
the necessary ecosystem – but then you have to deal
with the extreme climate. Therefore, look for dense
woodland comprising beech, ash and oak - a copse
won't help much in the long term.

You'll need fresh running water – a stream is better
than a river and a spring is best of all as it doesn't
need filtering. Always follow a stream as far back
as you can and see just what sort of land it passes
through before it reaches your retreat – farms can
poison a water supply through pesticide run off, and
cow and pig manure can make it toxic. If you suspect
really nasty things in your water then dig a well.
Bring in a dowser or try yourself.

You'll need a garden – about half an acre if you want to support a family or very small group. On that you'll grow everything apart from corn, which is why it's also a good idea to plant your retreat near an existing corn field. At some point you'll want bread and for that you'll need a lot of corn.

You'll soon discover the sheer amount of wood you need for warmth and cooking. Throwing a load of dead-fall logs on the campfire when you're only staying for the weekend is a completely different ball game to having a year-long supply of firewood. Ration your wood, season it, split it and you'll make it last longer while making it more useful. Trees take a long time to grow.

Choose a location which you can defend and which isn't easily accessible from a major road. At some point, other survivors are going to need to become more adventurous and you don't want unexpected visitors. People are quite predictable and will generally go for those resources close at hand or within visual range – if your retreat is tucked away several fields behind an abandoned railway line then it might never pop up on the radar (especially if your wood smoke isn't visible because you've used a disperser). The longer your retreat remains undiscovered the more likely you are to survive the first wave of cataclysm. Time equals less mouths.

Look for livestock. Be prepared to grab a beast, butcher and smoke or salt it in one go. The meat will last your group quite a long time (think one handful each per day). There are plenty of sheep on the moors. Ideally, you should be raising your own stock – chickens and goats are the hardiest and most useful. Check if there are any pheasant rearing pens in your vicinity, and if the fields have any rabbit warrens.

If you choose your retreat location properly, and do so before the SHTF, then you can prepare and stock it to fit your long-term needs. A good suggestion would be to bring in any material you need to build, etc. rather than using your local resources. Use planks while you can. Put in the hard work now and make your retreat as comfortable as possible. Don't restrict your thinking to just *survival* – get as luxurious as you can afford (just remember no electricity…).

Prepping requires sacrifice. You need to decide if you really need all those mod-cons like a new flat screen TV or a tablet computer now or if your money, and time, wouldn't be better invested in securing a future in an uncertain world. Preparing a self-sufficient homestead (put in solar panels or wind-turbine if you're electronically capable) means that in an economic crisis your family will have food, even if the world doesn't end.

Shelter

"Anyone who has spent a few nights in a tent during a storm can tell you: The world doesn't care all that much if you live or die."

—Anthony Doerr

My Bug Out Location has four walls and a roof; another's might have a sail; another's might be a plastic tarpaulin strung between some trees; another's might be a concrete box buried underground. Regardless of what type of BOL shelter you choose to fit your own personal needs, remember that shelter is one of the four primary necessities for survival (fire or warmth, water, food and shelter) so, at a minimum, it must be capable of keeping you out of the elements, the warmer and drier the better.

While in an ideal world we could all have a rustic cabin in the woods, don't be put off planning your shelter now just because luxury property is off your economic horizon.

Once you have chosen your BOL, concentrate on how you mean to live there for the fairly long term. If civilization does take a tumble, getting out of the city and setting up camp at your intended site will have to happen almost immediately. Calculate mobility into your plans plus any hidden factors which might mean you have to change them at a moment's notice. This lack of alternative, back-up planning is one that plagues the prepper's mindset. People get so preoccupied with one goal that they neglect to prepare for when plans go awry; this is especially seen in Bug In Locations. Think what you would need to do if your intended BOL and shelter are occupied by other survivors, or even destroyed. What's your Plan B? If you haven't already got one then start planning now. Your Little House on the Prairie, in which you'd hoped to live post-Doomsday, might get flattened, or infested by bandits, before you even arrive.

If you're going it alone then you have far more possibilities than if you're bringing family and friends and dog. A simple bivouac or hammock would suffice and both are light and easily transportable. For groups, look into getting one or more large tents and plan on, and practice, distributing the weight between you. Having the basic luxury of a canvas roof over your heads will give you breathing space while you discuss other options; expecting to find, or even build, a suitable house-like structure, unoccupied and in the ideal location immediately after a cataclysm might leave you huddling in the rain and cold.

Think outside the box. A country cottage for a BOL might be way too expensive where you live but might be affordable somewhere else. You don't need to wait till doomsday to move, you can make a life change now.

Think simple but keep your ambitions handy. Your primary aim will be to find or erect shelter; you can get more elaborate once you've learned the lay of the new landscape.

Having a portable canvas, or Spage-Age material, tent will relieve you of a huge amount of initial stress. Also, if you're a large group, you need to include other portable structures such as kitchen area, toilet, etc. Either that or know how, and have the materials, to build them. Tents get very claustrophobic when the rain won't let up. And don't forget all the extras which make camp life more comfortable – lighting, cooking utensils, seating, etc.

There are many arguments both for and against either canvas or nylon for tents. If you have a means of transporting it, and have a higher budget, then aim for the old military or scout type canvas tents as they're much more forgiving than the lighter, more modern nylon backpacking ones. They're also much easier to repair in a survival situation.

I've heard many preppers announce that they have caravans fully kitted out and plan to tow them to their planned BOLs. While a caravan *in situ* already at the BOL is several steps up from having a tent, it appears that those planning to tow one haven't factored in potential roadblocks. They would be wise, if that is their primary intention, to have at hand some other means of providing shelter, one which can be transported easily should they need to abandon their vehicles. A tent, for example...

Distance is a nagging detail in whatever form of shelter you set your heart on. If you're aiming for a permanent structure, how far away is it? Is it far enough away that it won't be mobbed by the crazed hordes, or is it too far away that you'd need to trek for days to reach it and require alternative forms of shelter *en route*. Having the perfect shelter five hours drive away, or even in another country, is just illogical. Try getting there on foot, with your entire intended party in tow, and see how long it takes you to reach it, what equipment you'll need to carry, and in what state you all are when you reach there. And don't stop at pubs or service stations on the way; imagine that the world's gone fully lights out and that the roads are filled with armed joyriders and burning wrecks. Does your post-apocalyptic

Dunroamin still seem the best option? If not, then swallow your pride and think again.

Remember, the aim at the most basic of levels is to keep you and your party out of the elements and somewhere where you won't be the targets of hungry, rapine thugs. Start your planning with that in mind, get that bit sorted and have that equipment ready to go, and only then begin contemplating your permanent base of operations.

If speed, evasion or even financial restraints are a major concern then make sure you at least have a sleeping bag, thermal blanket and emergency bivvy bag for each member of your party.

Sitting under a hedge, slowly dying from hypothermia as the winter rains lash down, might be too late to realize that that abandoned cottage you saw in the middle of Dartmoor last year whilst on holiday is probably a bit too far for your Gran to walk to.

Learn from Nature

"Forget not that the earth delights to feel your bare feet and the winds long to play with your hair."

—Kahlil Gibran

I walked up a rocky, dry and dusty track, up the hill that leads to the forest. The sun beat down, another record temperature day at 38 degrees Centigrade in the shade. The wind blew but merely teased, it did nothing to relinquish the heat. The ground was barren, the grass yellowed. Plantain stalks struggled to stand erect. All around me, crickets chirped and horse flies swarmed; apart from they, there was nothing. No animals, they were all hidden deep within the forest; the boar squelching in their muddy wallows.

Learning from nature is an essential aspect of prepping and bushcraft. Observing what wildlife does, and when, and understanding why, can vastly improve your chances of survival. If, on a hot day like that, with the sky utterly cloudless and the sun relentless, only a fool such as myself would decide to take a long, uphill walk. Conserving bodily fluids, maintaining a core body temperature of approximately 37 degrees, these are the primary aspects of survival. By placing yourself in a situation where you're having to compensate for the environment or the weather or other extremes means you're already at a disadvantage and, ultimately, fighting a losing battle. It is far better, then, to observe the animals in your area, and the birdlife, and note what they do at different times of the day and at different times of the night, and follow their lead.

We must understand wildlife in its natural habitat, even if that habitat is urban, such as with the fox, the pigeon, the starling, the sparrow or the rat. Many ancient tribes and warrior societies, such as the Aztecs, the Vikings, Shaolin monks and the Ninja, observed various animals and emulated them to achieve different ends.

The fox is known for its stealth and its cunning; a fox wandering down a road under the noon sun is ill. A healthy fox wouldn't dream of doing such a thing. It hunts at night, when it's cool and when it's dark. It skulks. Therefore, if you intend to move covertly, or your plan is to acquire something under dangerous conditions, then it is necessary to be as the fox. Think as the fox. Put yourself in the fox's position.

In the modern world, since the Age of Enlightenment, we've seen nature as being subservient to ourselves. We think we are the Masters of all. We laugh at the stupidity of animals because they cannot write or construct buildings, but this is because we are completely reliant on technology. Should we lose technology, then once again we shall find ourselves battling nature. Or, for the intelligent ones among us, adapting and living with the flow of nature.

> *"Earth is abundant with plentiful resources. Our practice of rationing resources through monetary control is no longer relevant and is counter-productive to our survival."*

> —Jacque Fresco

Nature can be a very cruel mistress. She can kill, easily, as anyone who has ever walked in the mountains or in the desert can attest. But she also provides a stunning bounty of fruit, fuel and food for those who learn to live with her instead of fighting against her. It is important to realize that while humans do have sentience and intelligence, we are still merely biological mechanisms on a planet spinning in circles in space, just as every other biological mechanism on Earth. Without oil or electricity on a huge scale we're forced to labour our sustenance from the soil or from what we can forage. A mixture of hunter-gatherer and agriculture. Without such encompassing technology, we become utterly reliant on the seasons.

In only the last few decades we have become used to going to a supermarket and buying products from far-flung places at any time of the year, and at reasonably cheap prices. Bananas, pomegranates, coconuts, melons, tobacco, cotton; we no longer see these goods as a luxury yet if the system should collapse we will find it extremely difficult to reproduce these goods in any quantity, certainly not for wholesale and, even then, only for the expert gardeners amongst us, and I definitely wouldn't include myself in that list.

By observing nature, we can learn what to eat and when. In the *Tao of Prepping*, I will not be going through lists of wild foods or crops which can be grown at home. There are many better and more comprehensive guides available for such topics. I merely wish the reader to take the time and understand and observe how the world changes, sometimes in minute details, sometimes in great natural upheavals. During these time frames, sometimes seasons, sometimes months, sometimes weeks, sometimes overnight even, by observing and planning for these changes we can be far more prepared than those reliant on store-based products.

For example, mushrooms. I'm not going to recommend that anybody go out into the forest or field and start harvesting fungi willy-nilly, not without expert guidance, but once some knowledge has been learned about which mushrooms are edible and at what times of the year, the clever will begin to observe weather patterns, predicting storms or rain, preparing for a dawn hike with basket in hand and sharp paring knife in pocket, to harvest this bounty of nature, remembering not to take the root, to slice cleanly, and not to take all the plants.

Freshly picked morrell mushrooms

By observing nature, and by knowing where the plants grow, you'll begin to realize that they often grow in the same location year after year, for decades and generations. By knowing the location, and by not over-cropping, and by following the seasons and changes in weather, you will quickly find your larder filled without having to use a store or credit card, or your hard-earned cash to replenish your stocks, merely by learning from nature.

Totem

"What is a totem: It is as a rule an animal (whether edible and harmless or dangerous and feared) and more rarely a plant or a natural phenomenon (such as rain or water)"

—Sigmund Freud

I stood beside a well-worn salt-lick, a quartz meteorite looking object, in a dry patch filled with boar prints and boar shit. Barely hidden in the tree line was a wooden hunting tower and, in the distance, endless hills and forests. Horseflies bit through my damp cotton shirt, attracted by the sweat. As I walked, the desiccated grass crisped and crumbled beneath my feet, and the cooling shade of the oak, birch, sycamore, beech and ash forest not yards from me beckoned.

The instant I passed the shade line I felt the temperature drop five, then ten degrees. There was much more herbage there, half of which I couldn't recognize. There are some books which have become almost universal among the prepping and bushcraft community, books which have stood the test of time and which are recommended to professionals and amateurs alike. I don't wish to go through lists of books and other items but I'd recommend everyone get themselves a copy of *Food for Free*, by Richard Mabey. I've carried a copy in one form or another, the large and pocket versions, for over two decades. My memory is not the greatest and while through practice and experience I have learned to identify certain wild foods, I still like to have an expert reference at hand just to confirm.

As I walked into the forest and the thick foliage overhead blocked out most of the sun, save for tiny glittering patches on some of the leaves and the floor beneath, I saw tracks and paths going in all directions, and I knew that just a few hours earlier, at dawn, these were packed highways of herds, packs and solitary hunters.

By learning basic tracking skills, and then understanding what the animal was thinking, what it was doing, where it was going, and from whence it came, allows you to really understand the animal kingdom and, by doing so, you have a much greater chance of putting food on the table.

Ancient peoples worshipped their food. They created elaborate rituals and decked their caves and temples with extensive artwork depicting successful hunts and powerful, healthy beasts. Each day they lived with this imagery, they adopted the animals as part of their own culture. In battle they wore their skins and took on the life force of the very beasts they hunted. It is important, very, very important therefore, to learn about nature and to learn your own totem.

It doesn't matter where you live, you could be in a high-rise block of flats, but you still have a connection to the beasts that roam the land, or fly in the air or swim in the water, or slither underfoot. Everyone has their own totem, a spirit guide somewhere between this world and the next, and it is important to learn what your totem is because through the totem you can gain access to the secret world of the animals. In some ways it is like a gate keeper, it opens the door.

When I was very young, six or seven years old, I was camping with my parents near the New Forest. One day we went for a walk in the New Forest, along a marked trail. I remember it as being a hot day. I was wearing sandals and shorts. Suddenly, I felt something move onto my foot, something slithered. It was cold and I could feel its heart beating through my skin. I looked down and there was an adder. It had crossed halfway across my foot and stopped and it lay there, resting, panting. My parents were shocked and told me not to move, so I didn't. I don't know how long it remained there, memory has a means of confusing time, but it was perfectly peaceful and it eventually slithered off from right to left across the path, off into the bracken and ferns. I was shocked, absolutely stunned.

A large brown female adder

A few hours later, we were back at the campsite and my mother was cooking on an open fire. She had a huge pan of boiling water, presumably for soup or stew or something. She'd warned me repeatedly not to go near the fire but, being quite an active youth, I ignored her and ran past. I kicked over the pan of boiling water onto my foot, the same foot the adder had recently rested on. The boiling water scolded my skin to the point where it bubbled and began falling off. I lost all the skin on my foot, and each day for weeks afterwards I had to go to the nearest hospital to have the doctors pop hot water blisters and to remove all the remaining destroyed skin. The pain was agonizing.

The skin on my foot has since grown back, and hasn't even left a noticeable scar. The adder, my totem or my omen, had either warned me about the impending disaster or it had cursed me, I don't know which, but throughout my life, and in many different countries on different continents, I've come into contact with various vipers. I've hunted them,

I've eaten them, I've skinned them and I've worn them as armbands and belts, and still, occasionally, one will cross my path out of the blue and just sit there, resting in front of me and allow me to take photographs before it peacefully wanders off.

Baby smooth snake

We've even had baby adders come pouring through cracks in the skirting board at the house, followed by a baby smooth snake; snakes regularly nest under the gable and they, upon hatching, must have headed to the relative warmth. The Chinese believe that having a writhing floor brings good luck.

Luck and fortune may also be predicted depending on whether your totem, or a black cat in its stead, crosses your path from left to right, which is good, or from right to left, which is bad.

Not everyone will have such an extreme introduction to their totem, or their omen, but everyone has one.

The best way of finding your totem, if they haven't introduced themselves to you personally, is to just close your eyes while in a peaceful place, without distractions. Imagine your ideal place, the natural location where you feel most at peace and in

harmony with nature, and just breathe slowly in and
out and allow your mind to drift. Whatever animal
comes first, and takes you with it, is likely to be your
omen, or totem. It may not be what you were hoping
for but you'll see what I mean if you let yourself go
with the flow of it.   Wolves, eagles, falcons, bears,
ravens, even pygmy shrews and a myriad of other
creatures may appear in your vision to guide you;
chances are you probably already have an inkling as
to what awaits beyond the veil. However, should you
be greeted by a big black dog then you might want
to pull back to reality and analyse any potential
current dangers in your life...

Dogs, Cats and Other Beasties

"If you pick up a starving dog and make him prosperous he will not bite you. This is the principal difference between a dog and man."

—Mark Twain

Dogs

Truly Man's (and Woman's) best friend, having a dog means you'll at least have one living thing you can trust when all around you has gone postal. Alright, so it's another mouth to feed but unless your survival strategy is based on stealth and evasion, a dog might just save your bacon.

In terms of true survival, a mixed-breed mutt is much less likely to get ill, die young, or develop any of the innumerable debilitating disorders which rack up vet fees in more pedigree breeds. However, pedigree breeds were bred for specific purposes and if you buy from a reputable, established breeder (as opposed to a backyard puppy farm) your little pooch should grow up to do what it said on the label – with a lot of training.

First things first, though, know why you need the dog and what its purpose will be – every mouth will have to earn its keep so try not letting your 6 year old daughter do the choosing, as a Chihuahua or Red Setter might not be the most useful option, regardless of how cute they look as puppies.

For survival purposes there are three main types of dog – hunting, guard and alarm. There is a fourth type, herding, which would be useful in a long-term or traditional living scenario where you'll be at the livestock raising phase but you're more likely to need a flock guard than a sheep dog unless you're breeding large numbers of woolly meat racks.

Hunting

This can be split into two categories – dogs which hunt and dogs which support the hunt. Whippets, lurchers, greyhounds, wolfhounds, basically anything with hound in its name, will run down rabbit and hare. They're also generally thinner and lankier than other breeds which means they'll eat less than a guard dog. No Yorkshire poacher would be seen *up ont moor bar whippet*. If you're not planning on shooting or trapping then these breeds might be the way to go.

The second category is what could also be termed sporting dogs – Labradors, pointers, spaniels, and retrievers. Basically you shoot and they fetch. Only really useful if large bodies of water feature in your survival plan and you don't like getting wet.

Guarding

There's nothing quite like a large lump of muscle and teeth to dissuade an intruder. Thanks again to the Nanny State, several breeds have been made unavailable (including my personal favourite, the American Bandog, which is half pitbull, half mastiff) which excel at guarding, or have been so diluted by the Kennel Club show-ring that they are, to all intents and purposes, useless. A guard dog's job is to deter and defend – it puts people, and other creatures, off coming into your protected area and it takes down the stupidly persistent. Don't confuse a dog with a loud bark with one that will get the job done – tenacity can be trained (or at least developed) into an animal but it is usually present from birth (which is why there are renowned bloodlines).

Rottweilers are literally the dog's bollocks when it comes to guarding, and probably the best available for the purpose in the UK. However, for those with kids I wouldn't recommend them. A better alternative for the survivalist family would be an English Bullmastiff or Boxer, although never leave any dog alone with little children. All *molossers* (the big-headed, big-bodied breeds) are good at guarding if for nothing more than their sheer size and intimidation factor. On the whole, they're generally lazy, phlegmatic and extremely hard headed, which can make them difficult to train. But they eat a lot.

Veles

Choose a breed depending on your plans and individual character. If you're aiming to stash yourself away and not move around much then get an English Bullterrier. If you've got a bit more land then choose a molosser. If you're planning on doing quite a bit of roaming then an Akita Inu or Rhodesian Ridgeback. Probably the best all-round dogs, and the easiest to train, are the German Shepherd (the Belgian Malinois is a smaller, meaner version) and the Border Collie.

One excellent tip is to train your guard dog its commands in a foreign language - you can find various training vocabularies online. This will stop a confident intruder from commanding your dog as it won't understand him. This trick is often used by police and border agencies around the world.

Alarm dogs

These are also good for vermin removal as often that is what they were originally designed for. These would be a secondary dog, a sort of side-kick for your main, much larger, hunting or guard dog. Most terriers will happily rip up a rat, and when the sewerage system switches off you're going to get a lot of them. Often, a larger molosser will wait until a potential intruder is but a few feet away before bothering to get up and go sort out the problem, leaving you little chance to prepare. A terrier will start yapping and panicking if a bat farts half a mile away and will let you know instantly. In their role as support dog, they'll also make damned sure that their larger partner heeds the call much quicker than they'd otherwise like.

There are many potential breeds of alarm dog to choose from but on this I'd recommend a mutt as they're much hardier and will do the job just as well – just don't get a toy or lap breed.

Dogs are an extremely important psychological aid for long-term survival. They quickly become close friends and, if treated well, will remain loyal. If you have kids then caring for the dog can be an excellent

Sandy

means of transferring their stress and trauma from a SHTF scenario into a productive and educational function. Plus, hearing your own personal guard snoring heavily next to you at night removes a lot of tension from an unpredictable environment.

On a more negative note, the chances are high that, post-SHTF, there will be packs of feral dogs roaming the land. Romania has had this problem for decades and there is no cure in sight. Learn dog behaviour and training and perhaps plan to carry some form of deterrent, akin to pepper spray, when these packs become a daily hazard.

Cats

*"Owners of dogs will have noticed that, if you provide
them with food and water and shelter and affection,
they will think you are god. Whereas owners of cats
are compelled to realize that, if you provide them
with food and water and shelter and affection, they
draw the conclusion that they are gods."*

—Christopher Hitchens

If you're Bugging In for the long term then you need
one. Just don't expect your pet moggy to switch
from cat food on a plate to hunting rodents. If you
want a cat for vermin control then raise one as such.
Also, make damned sure it's spayed or neutered
otherwise your house will either quickly become a
kitten farm or will stink from where the tom has
sprayed his presence. One major downside of having
a feline companion when civilization takes a tumble
is that antibiotics and other medications will become
scarce and cats can carry several quite dangerous
infections which are transferable to humans, such
as bartonellosis (cat scratch disease), salmonellosis
(diarrhea, fever, cramps), cryptosporidiosis, and
toxoplasmosis, not to mention ringworm and cat flu.
These only really become an issue when hygiene
isn't maintained or when you let your cat decorate
your home with its faeces but in a survival situation
hygiene will deteriorate due to the lack of water and
sanitation.

I've heard several survivalists say that they've eaten
cat. I say good luck to them as you'd never catch me
doing so. Firstly, they're one of the most intelligent
species on this planet and secondly they can carry

way too many nasty parasites inside them. The same goes for fox.

Other creatures

At some point you'll probably eat your pet iguana, python, tarantula, budgies and anything else you can get your hands on. Ferrets (and polecats) are extremely useful for rabbiting but only if you've had a lot of experience with them, e.g. born and raised. They bite and they stink. Best kept outside in a fortified rabbit hutch. Falconry is a survivalist's dream and for most of us it will have to remain so. If you're really thinking along those lines (Kes!) then start learning now or, better yet, 5 years ago. Chances are you'd probably end up eating it anyway.

Bush Kit

"The Wilderness holds answers to more questions than we have yet learned to ask."

—Nancy Wynne Newhall

A particularly large wood ant bit the flesh of my lower back and reminded me that I wasn't the boss of the forest. I was surrounded by birch trees; some dead, some not, some fallen, some rotten. The wind rustled the leaves above as it passed through and a Jay shrieked up in the tree tops. I could hear large things moving a few hundred yards away but because of the dense foliage and undergrowth I couldn't see what they were.

Out here, when you enter a forest or walk through it, unless you're specifically hunting, you talk loudly, you make noise, because you want the game to know you're there so that you don't surprise them. It gives them a chance to get out of the way. Walking into a group of boar sows and piglets, or a pack of wolves, or a bear, and surprising them as they're resting from the afternoon heat is not a clever thing to do.

In the forest, regardless of how hot it might be, I always wear full length trousers and long sleeved shirt, and high leg boots. I've met many people who wear shorts, T-shirt and sandals because it's a pleasant day outside. What they don't realize is that inside the forest there are many creatures which bite and sting, and many plants which do also.

A red squirrel walked directly in front of me and jumped across low hanging branches. He hadn't seen me and, because of wind direction, it appeared he couldn't smell me either. A tiny little thing foraging for nuts on the few hazel trees around. It was nice to have company of the gentle kind.In the forest, the floor crawls with biting creatures. Here, in particular, the wood ant is king. It doesn't seem as though there is a single inch free, throughout the entire forest, from these giant biting creatures which manage to get inside your clothes or on your face or neck.

In the leaves, ticks hang, and in the long grasses, waiting for a passing animal or human. Simply tucking your trousers into your socks helps prevent them from crawling up your legs into more private locations where they're likely to go unnoticed until much later and where they'll already have become deeply buried in your flesh. Ticks carry nasty diseases – *encephalitis, borreliosis* – so it's important

Forget the nice and new in the bush - equip yourself with hard-wearing, easily repairable gear which, if you break or lose it, you won't need to spend a small fortune to replace. Deer and trees don't care about brand names, neither should you. The long-handled, small-headed axe is the traditional Slovak shepherd's tool/weapon, the Valaska. *They're easy to make and are the ideal, multi-purpose walking stick*

to keep covered up. And then there are the swarms of deer-louse-flies and horseflies...

As for mosquitoes, pray that you're not male, sweaty and with O-blood-group as recent studies claim that's their primary target. Lucky, lucky me...

I always wear a hat or a headscarf. During the summer it's to keep the sun off of my face and neck, and to stop sweat from dripping into my eyes, stinging them. In the winter it's to keep me warm.

While it has become popular over recent years due
to certain television programmes to go barefoot, I
would never recommend this, nor would I venture
into the bush with anyone who did so. Boots mean
that you don't have to constantly watch on what
you're treading. While eventually, and with practice,
you can learn to move fairly quietly over twigs and
grass and through brush in boots, you shouldn't be
spending your entire time having to look down to
see on what your feet are stepping. A simple thorn
in the underside of your foot can lead to infection,
especially if, a few moments later, you step in dirty
water in which an animal has urinated, defecated, or
even died and rotted. In a post-cataclysmic situation,
where modern medicines and antibiotics become
scarce, the slightest wound can lead to tragedy, as it
did just a hundred years ago.A stout, waterproof pair
of boots means you can walk in the dark without
worrying. Good luck trying to find the perfect
pair for you, though; it's one of the Holy Grails of
prepping.

Some people go over the top with what they take into
the bush, and others are too minimalistic. There is
a healthy balance. If you carry too much you become
quickly exhausted and I guarantee you're unlikely to
use much of what you carry.

There is an illusion in prepping that you must be
prepared for everything, but you must also use logic
and common sense. On a hot day you will need to
bring more water than on a cool day, but even on a
cool day you'll still need to bring water.

The black, bulky body of a raven flew overhead, its
partner pursuing. Their throaty croaks continued to
haunt long after they'd passed me.

Many preppers develop an obsession for boots, bags and knives - nothing is ever 'just right', which means having to try again, and again. As such, many preppers end up with cupboards full of boots, bags and knives...

Always bring food when going into the bush. Sometimes you can walk further than you originally intended, or the climate might be more exacting than you'd predicted, and you burn off calories. I often find myself feeling dizzy and needing chocolate or sugar or anything sweet after chopping wood or digging for several hours, or even just going on a long hike – this is due to having not eaten enough healthy food beforehand. Carrying some trail mix, or meat jerky, can really help. In the bush, unlike in a desk job, calories are king.

There are lots of items of *tacticool* kit which are the latest design or the latest fashion, extremely expensive, lots of which I would like and if I had the money I would go out and buy endless supplies of the stuff, but I'd probably never use most of it. I have a few items at home which are expensive – a bag, a certain machete, a jacket, a knife – and I'd never dream of taking them into the bush because they're too nice.

Imagine that when you go out to reconnect with nature, that nature isn't as warm and embracing as you think. Nature has holes, sharp bits, mud, little things that stick out in unexpected places. Dress as though you wouldn't care if you had to throw away your clothes after you returned from the bush; the intent is not to but don't dress in brand new kit.

Carry a bag which you don't mind getting rips in, an old canvas satchel with a bit of waterproofing and which can be easily repaired. Don't take a several hundred pound knife which you could easily lose or break, take a cheaper one which can take a beating but if you misplace it somewhere in the dense leaf matter you're not going to cry about it. Keep the shiny things at home, if you really need them in the first place.

I'm a great believer in recycling and reusing. Ideally, you should be able to get all of your bush kit in second hand stores, charity shops or as hand-me-downs. If you have children, this should be your first port-of-call anyway. Don't buy new boots and clothes for your kids to go out to the bush, as they'll only outgrow them and you'll have to do it again and again and thus waste money, another major resource. There are charity shops on every high street, some of which stock amazing brand name clothing and equipment for pennies. No one has to know where you bought your kit. This isn't a fashion parade, it's about survival – both in the long term and in the short economic term. It's about being prepared in harsh environments and for disasters.

Use your kit, practice with it. All those items you have still in their original packaging you may as well toss away now. If you haven't put it all through extreme conditions then you have no idea if it will be useful or just dead weight.

Sometimes the simplest things are best.

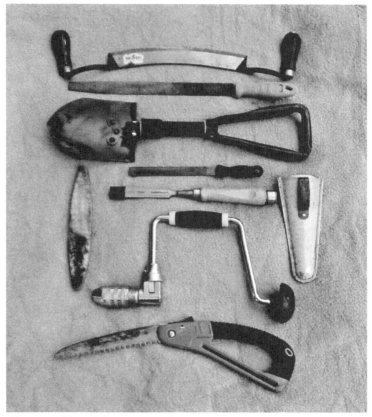

Extra stuff used for campcraft

Tao of Prepping

Fire

"He who plays with fire may become its victim"

—Chinese proverb

In the modern world it is becoming increasingly rare to find locations where you can have an open fire and, with modern food and equipment, it isn't even really necessary. A fire is for warmth and for cooking, and with modern equipment both of these can be performed by, often better, alternatives. Having good clothing and a tent will provide warmth and shelter, and many foods are instantly edible just by opening a packet. Should the SHTF, then open fires will again become *de rigeur*, but in the current world no.

Yes, carry a lighter and a fire starting kit for extreme emergencies but if you're only going a few miles from town to a copse of woods next to a road, then you're only deluding yourself that such an emergency could arise where you would need to light a fire.

However, it is essential that you do learn and practice how to light a fire and sustain one under different conditions. Learn how to start one without a lighter or matches if you're able. But, once you've learned, refrain from doing so.

Fire is one of the most mystical, hypnotizing elements in our world and, while the physics of its creation are understood, the elemental itself still isn't. Fire is a living thing which can heat, cook, burn and kill. It is an extremely powerful and hungry spirit and our lighting of it is little more than a ritual to call it into our realm. Fire must be fed or it dies; it must be strictly controlled or it will grow and run amok. Like humans, it needs fuel, heat and oxygen to survive.

Always dig a fire pit and clear the area of leaves, twigs and other flammable material. Make sure there are no overhanging branches. Make one person responsible for tending the fire and prevent others from tossing on more logs than are needed. Never burn plastics – always pack rubbish away and take it home with you. Let the fire burn clean, especially if you intend to cook on it. Always stock twice as much wood as you think you'll need, especially before nightfall – you don't want to run out in the dark.

Lighting fires all over the place, especially illegally, will just place the entire prepping and bushcraft community under further restrictions. If you're not in a place where it is entirely permitted, or if it isn't completely necessary, then don't do it. If you need to cook something, then use a small, and I mean small, fire, cook your food then extinguish the fire afterwards. Don't build massive bonfires just to boil a kettle. Start conserving resources now, and dead-fall firewood is one of the most important.

When you've finished with your fire, make sure it is completely out and then fill in the fire-pit. Make the ground look as though you were never there.

The Knife

"Fill your bowl to the brim and it will spill. Keep sharpening your knife and it will blunt."

—Lao Tzu

Plastic bottles hanging on string surrounding my neighbour's vegetable patch rattled as a dust devil blew in from the parched hillside. Even though there'd been a storm a few days earlier, with a lot of hard hitting heavy rain, the ground had been so dry that instead of soaking up the much needed moisture, most of the fallen water had run off into gullies or through cracks in the soil and again the ground was dry. A lone Red hind, little more than a fawn, grazed those shoots strong enough to survive the unusual weather. My dog barked at her and she bolted.

Probably the single most discussed topic in the prepping and bushcraft community concerns what knife is the knife to have, and there are almost as many opinions as there are preppers. The old saying 'three is two, two is one and one is none' also applies where knives are concerned so most people double up in case one gets lost or broken. This has led many to favour cheaper knives.

Many preppers would also count themselves collectors where blades are concerned, buying far more than is really necessary and of many different types. Then there are the various bags in which a knife features as part of the ready kit – EDC, GHB, BOB – which means having more than one is necessary.

Three common types of pocket knife. The one in the middle, the lock knife, is illegal to carry in the UK; the one on the left, the Balisong or Butterfly knife, is illegal even to possess. And to carry the one on the right, the SAK, you must have a plausible reason.

In terms of true usability, as opposed to the more exotic curios which wind up in collections, there are three main types: the pen knife, the multi-tool (not strictly a knife but they do have blades), and a belt or sheath knife. Both pen knives and multi-tools have folding blades and belt knives generally have fixed blades. Knowing where a knife is to be carried often dictates its type, according to law, but that's not to say the perfect blade can't be tucked securely away at home for use post-SHTF, unless that too breaks the law (flick, gravity and butterfly knives in the UK are illegal even in the home). Make sure you know what you're legally allowed to carry, even own, where you live before you go out and start spending your hard earned cash.

For the sake of argument, we'll imagine that you don't want to carry any knife in public and instead magically appear at your campsite with it, or them. And that campsite is on private land where you have full rights and permission to both camp and carry sharp objects. If you've never actively used a sharp blade before then seek instruction first. There is never any shame in learning from an expert, especially where safety is concerned.

Each type of knife has its own supporters, often depending on the situation in which it will be used or the task it will be used for. Many penknives, especially the SAK or Swiss Army Knife variety, have multiple tools for doing small and delicate jobs but are no use for heavy work. A multi-tool is basically an SAK with a set of pliers attached. Similarly, fixed blades are generally designed to do heavier tasks but often aren't as useful when delicacy is required, nor do they have multiple tools although they do have multiple functions.

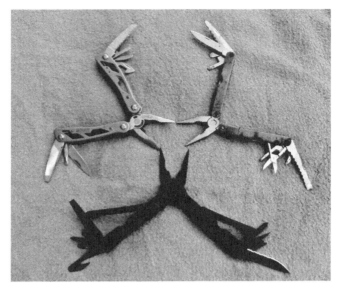

Multi-tools range from the very cheap and instantly breakable (the Chinese model, top right), to the affordable and sturdy (the Stanley, top left), to the ludicrously expensive and almost indestructible, (the SOG, bottom, cheers Pete...)

Equipping yourself with a good penknife and a good fixed blade is the best way to go, and use them for what each does best. With penknives, don't skimp on the price. Buying a cheap copy of an SAK or multi-tool will ultimately result in you being left with a dud at a very inopportune moment. Many preppers double up on their SAK by also having a single-bladed folder, often a lock knife. There are a wide variety to choose from, from many different manufacturers. Experience with use will help you decide which is right for you. Buy because it feels right, not because it's fashionable.

When it comes to fixed blades, there are some who prefer the cheaper Scandinavian type knives and there are those who invest in custom-made hand-forged ones; sometimes it's the price which dictates the choice, and sometimes experience. Always consider the fact that knives can break or be misplaced, especially when used at night.

Disregarding the price, which is a personal issue, there are a couple of very important aspects which you need to address when choosing a fixed blade. The first is the tang. This is the bit of the blade which continues into the handle.   Many cheaper knives don't have a full tang, which means the blade doesn't reach the end of the handle, which would give it more strength, and instead finish only a third or half way through. This is also an important factor in a survival situation where the handle may break and need to be replaced – it is far easier to repair a full tang than a half. Many fixed blades sold as *'Rambo'* or *'Survival'* knives often have virtually no tang whatsoever as they have hollow handles to store a minuscule 'survival kit'. These are generally cheap imitations of extremely expensive one-piece metal knives where the lack of tang is made up for in the overall construction. Steer clear of cheap survival knives.

There are many blade types, from curved to straight, from saw-back to front-weighted; try to let practicality rather than cool design affect your decision. Often, the most complicated looking knives are the least useful whereas a simple, straight blade with full tang and riveted wooden handle will last you the longest and serve its purpose better. Also, while it may not have the intimidation factor of a giant crocodile knife or Bowie, a shorter, fatter blade will be more useful for most camp craft – and easier and lighter to both carry and use.

The next major factor when choosing a blade is deciding between carbon steel and stainless. Both have their pros and cons – carbon is easier to sharpen and stays sharp longer, but it also rusts whereas stainless steel doesn't. If you intend using your knife around water then always go with stainless. Unless you're a hardcore bushman and plan on using your knife almost as often as you breathe, then go with stainless. It will make life a lot easier. Carbon steel is very useful in larger blades such as machetes and swords because it is more forgiving, more flexible and less brittle than stainless but in shorter blades such as knives, you need a certain amount of rigidity.

Some machete types

Make sure your knife has a decent sheath. If your perfect blade doesn't come with one then either buy another sheath, have one made or, ideally, make your own. The sheath must be able to prevent both the point and the blade of the knife from piercing or slicing through, which could cause you a grievous injury. It should also have a means to securely hold it, either in its near entirety or a tight clasp just above the hilt. Sheaths which have clasps too high up the handle, towards the pommel, allow too much free movement, meaning you could possibly lose your knife or even end up slicing yourself as you walk.

Just as the *katana* was to the samurai, so the knife is to the prepper and bushcrafter. It's a personal choice, and a personal statement. Chances are, you'll go through several different types, finding faults with each, until you come to your ideal one. Most old timers carried something akin to a carbon-bladed butcher's knife with a wooden handle, in a home-made sheath. I've seen some of these after decades of use where their blades have been sharpened so often over the years that they've lost almost half their belly but are still going strong. Money doesn't mean anything over hard-wearing practicality.

Ultimately, the best blade you ever own will be the one you make for yourself, either by grinding down an old file, or by hammering it out on a forge. This should be the aim of all who wish to be self-reliant.

Tao of Prepping

EDC and Scrip

"If you got something you don't want other people to know, keep it in your pocket."

—Muddy Waters

Made famous by Bernard Capulong's simple but excellent blog, and now the buzzword of survivalists the world over, the EDC (everyday carry) is something everyone should consider deeply. Basically, it's what you have on your person (pockets, belt, wrists, neck, purse) as you go about your daily life. If you're new to the survival field then empty all your pockets onto a table and have a look at how your EDC currently stands. Most people will probably have a wallet and keys and perhaps some receipts, loose change and some chewing gum.

Now imagine you're at work in your office on the 29th floor when a giant coronal mass ejection wipes out the electric grid and puts us back in the Dark Ages. Your EDC should be enough to get you home, where you can pick up your BOB, or Bug Out Bag, and head out to your retreat. Looking at the contents of your pockets before you, can you honestly say it's enough?

In an ideal world we'd carry our BOBs with us wherever we went, but the average Joe really doesn't get the concept of prepping so it would attract more than just a few stares. So you need to do this as clandestinely as possible. Think like a ninja. Be the Grey Man. The aim is for you to be capable of surviving in the short term whilst being able to pass unnoticed in daily life. That means wearing a machete on your belt is a no-no, as is webbing.For the sake of argument we'll imagine you have to wear a suit to earn your daily bread. It doesn't take much to distort the fit of a suit and that would be counter-productive, so you need to load up on items which don't weigh a lot and which won't create awkward lumps. I won't list the items here as that's not my intent. Take some time and research what fits your lifestyle best. With those few items you're ready to roll. But with a little extra space you can greatly increase your short term survival and for that you'll need a bag, a GHB, or Get Home Bag. Ideally, a *scrip* (the medieval term for a messenger bag or manbag; they also used to be called bread bags).

Knapsacks don't go well with suits, and briefcases incapacitate one of your hands, so invest in a scrip.

Church statue of a medieval pilgrim with scrip

Choose a large and hardy, leather and canvas one
– modern fashion dictates that you'll look *in* whilst
having a smaller version of the BOB at hand at all
times. Keep it visibly for your work needs – perhaps
create a false bottom, or have a zipped area for your
survival goods. Always think Grey Man.It's your
scrip so fill its secret cavity with what you think
you'll need. Research GHBs for a better idea of what
to carry. Keep within the law as you'll be carrying
it in pre-Apocalyptic times, and keep your EDC
surreptitious. Blend in.

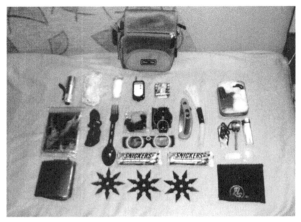

An example of a GHB and contents

Just another tourist in the crowd. Is that a camera case or a GHB?

Grey Man

"The best live among us in disguise."

—Louis Dudek

Military kit is designed for hard wearing, which is why it is often preferred by the prepping and bushcraft communities. Jungle issue lightweight DPM trousers are ideal for the heat, and are my current favourites for wearing in the summer bush – I'm still getting used to wearing adventurous polyamide trousers. But there is something about military kit which makes the prepper and bushcrafter into something we're not. We're not trying to recreate *Rambo*, and anyone who is is just deluding themselves that they're into bushcraft and prepping. The same goes for carrying

huge knives when it is definitely not necessary.
A three or four inch bladed steel hunting knife is
more than enough for what you'll ever encounter.
Carrying a twelve-inch, serrated, cheap Jimmy Lile
copy is just extra weight and is likely to get you
arrested, until such a time when law doesn't mean
anything.

Stealth and evasion, camouflage, are these really
necessary for the modern times? Ask yourself from
who are you hiding? Why would you need full
camouflage and a ghillie suit? Unless you're shooting
rabbits or stalking deer, or illegally camping on
someone's land.

There is a growing argument for the Grey Man
in the prepping and bushcraft community, and
the Grey Man may mean the difference between
our community being ostracised and eventually
criminalized, and in being accepted. If you need a
new rucksack, don't get one in camouflage colours,
get dark subdued colours instead – blues, blacks,
greys, greens, browns – but not in a military pattern.
Most animals aren't colour blind, but they can't
tell if you're wearing orange and black or black and
green; they just see two different colours. Movement,
noise, smell and silhouette are what spook them. If
you're hiking in the mountains, then go for brighter
colours; it means you're more likely to get rescued,
whereas wearing camouflage means that the
rescue party might not see you when you're lying
unconscious.

Green is the traditional colour for the forest
(bizarrely, deer can see greens and yellows) but our
ancestors wore a virtual kaleidoscope of colours also,
yellows and scarlets and blues. The material the

clothing is made from, and the quality of the fabric and stitching and seams, is of far more importance than its camouflage scheme.

The Grey Man means if you walk down the street you don't stand out like a potential home-grown terrorist. Imagine walking along the road carrying a military rucksack, wearing camouflage jacket and trousers, and big black army boots – the police would automatically stop you because it suggests to them that you're also carrying a weapon. If you walk down the road wearing lightweight hiking trousers, some brown hiking boots and gaiters, a Ripstop anorak and a 30 litre camping-brand backpack, they will think you're going hiking, a popular, encouraged and legal activity. Yes, you could have a small penknife on you but you're unlikely to be on your way to siege the local government offices.

Part of prepping and bushcraft is camouflage – don't get me wrong, this is an essential factor – whether in the bush, hunting for an animal, or whether it's just blending in to any environment, even urban. But by blending in you must blend in. A rambler blends in, a *Rambo* wannabe does not. Always think about your environment.

Perhaps if you're planning to find a location for a Bug Out, you should first visit or recce, sit in a local café and watch how the local hikers, cyclists and outdoor tourists are dressed, and then emulate them. Each area has its own idiosyncrasy, it could be a certain colour of raincoat, even a brand. If it's North Face and orange, go find one in charity shop or on E-bay. You can have your camouflage bush clothes in your bag, rolled up, or even worn underneath, but if you're walking through town on the way to your BOL, dress like the locals. And you'd be surprised just how much kit you can fit in a fashionable scrip...

Blend in.

Don't wear knives on your belt, even multi-tools in little pouches, unless you're deep in the bush. There's no need to. Don't carry a machete. Again, there's no need to. You're not in the jungles of the Philippines. Most experienced preppers and bushcrafters realize that a small camping axe, a folding saw, a small carbon bladed sheath knife or even just a folding knife, are more than sufficient for most camp craft. Carrying a zombie slaying machete will just have you put away, locked behind metal and concrete, the exact opposite of what you originally wished for.

> *"Conserving energy and thus saving money, reducing consumption of unnecessary products and packaging and shifting to a clean-energy economy would likely hurt the bottom line of polluting industries, but would undoubtedly have positive effects for most of us."*
>
> —David Suzuki

Reuse things. Don't buy new. Our resources are dwindling. The fashion industry tells us that last season's is shit and that we need this season's or even next season's. For most of the time, this is just nonsense. People wear their clothes, their boots, they carry their bags, their tents, for a few days in the field and then toss them away the following year to buy the latest versions. Hunt around for bargains, you'll find that you can kit your entire family out with good quality equipment for the price of a few, little better but technologically more modern, tacticool pieces of kit.

Psychology

"Our greatest weakness lies in giving up. The most certain way to succeed is always to try just one more time."

—Thomas Edison

"If you're going through hell, keep going."

—Winston Churchill

One of the main differences between the modern prepping movement and the old survivalist one is that it's not so much about the lone wolf and more about trying to keep your family alive when disasters arise. Once you've sorted out the basic survival elements of shelter, warmth, food and water, not necessarily in that order, you'll need to focus on psychology. After a few weeks of sitting in a cellar or tent, eating boiled rice and drinking wild herbal tea, chances are that both boredom and friction will be simmering, if not overflowing, amongst your party.

Keeping an active, positive mind is essential.

There are a few simple steps to keeping your group mentally healthy. Obviously, it's unlikely that you'll manage to prevent them talking about whatever caused their situation and its future implications, which could bring up some deep emotional anguish especially if loved ones have been harmed or lost, or their home has been destroyed, but by careful redirection you can turn this into a psychological asset. The key is in transforming negative thoughts such as "Woe is me! All is lost" to "Okay, the situation isn't great but we did prepare somewhat for it, unlike others. What can we do to make our lives better?"

Have both short term and long term goals – the more realistic and attainable the better. Fantasy can have a negative impact when it becomes clear that whatever you've been discussing is nigh on impossible, such as "Wouldn't it be great if we could go back to the good old days before the event happened".

Giving each member of the group a role in whatever activities you undertake, and supporting, even complimenting them, can give hope where before there was none. Many pensioners complain that the worst part of getting old is feeling useless after working all their lives, and many give up the will to live. The same applies in disaster psychology.

A group with nothing to do day after day will just dwell on the negative and slowly fall apart.

Short term goals could include building structures necessary for the group's daily life, bringing a sense of homeliness and civilization to their situation. Splitting the group into work details, dependent on their age, ability and fitness or health level, and having them go off foraging, wood collecting, wombling or hunting, both provides for the group as a whole – something seen in tribes the world over – and utilizes each member to the group's advantage.

Idle hands are the Devil's tools.

Ideally, your group should be somewhat physically exhausted at the end of each day, and be content to sit around the campfire and tell tales or recount amusing observations or concerns or future plans which have arisen during their work details.

For longer term goals, finding a better BOL, building a more permanent and defensible settlement, relationships and so on will keep the group thinking beyond their daily bread. Soap opera episodes end on a cliff hanger for a reason. For your group's sanity, always make sure that there's something over the horizon to look forward to or work towards.

Another means of dispelling boredom is with games. If you are prepping for two people or more, board games such as chess, scrabble or draughts are essential. Make the games competitive, keep a tally. Refer to previous games in conversation to keep the competition alive. Cards are an excellent means of uniting a group, just make sure that they don't bet with anything other than valueless objects such as twigs or leaves otherwise you may end up splitting the group. Traditionally, accusations of cheating in money-based card games ended very badly for at least one player; duelling is something you really want to avoid.

Musical instruments will really come back in force when the lights go out and are a good means of occupying people's minds in the evening. Prep for a shindig and include, or make, a few triangles or tambourines in case someone isn't musically talented – it will include them in the activity. Mouth organs, tin whistles, and recorders are all light and easy to stash in amongst your kit. A bongo drum can be improvised, as can my personal favourite, the *didgeridoo* – a drain pipe or a vacuum cleaner tube works well, just make sure you clean it first.

Encourage singing, dancing and story telling. The Saxons used to live together in large groups, sometimes including several different families, under one roof. One of their favourite activities was telling each other their dreams and then the others would then try to interpret them.

Keeping traditions, commemorating events and people, and ritualising certain aspects of life, has always been a major factor in human history. Always celebrate birthdays and traditional holidays, even create your own. Basically, anything which can unify your family or group is good, anything which splits the party is bad.

Ideally, you'll know everyone you're with personally, and will recognize the signs of depression or dissent. Deal with both quickly or they will spread. If you notice that one person is the attitude version of Typhoid Mary then distract and encourage them so that they channel their negative drive into something a lot more positive.

When it comes to a party of mixed acquaintance – some who know each other and others who are strangers – try to unite them as quickly as possible. They must share good times and bad together before they'll see each other as one unit. Create problems for the group to deal with but to which you already know the solution. Monitor them and make sure they don't make a mountain out of a molehill. Step in and resolve the issue if they don't manage to do so themselves but allow them the leeway to suffer a bit of stress together. Use your imagination.

If you do end up with one or more bad apples in the party, especially an antagonist with a penchant for shit stirring, try to speak to them alone and change their way of thinking by explaining the benefits of being part of a mentally, physically and spiritually healthy clan. If they persist in causing trouble and dividing your group then you'll need to deal with them more severely. In many tribes around the world, 'ghosting' is the worst punishment that can be given out and, for a tribesperson, it is the worst they could receive. It is where the tribe turns their back on them and they no longer exist. They are forced out the tribe and never allowed to return. Their name is never again mentioned and anything they owned is burned or destroyed. It is as though they never existed. As people don't generally live long in the wilds on their own, this was also a death sentence, albeit a slow one of starvation or from disease.

It may be necessary to be particularly harsh and theatrical when dealing with the first serious offender in your group. It will send a clear message to the others on many different levels.

Prepping is not just about the body, but also the mind and the spirit. Take all three into account when planning for the future.

The Yeoman

"A yeoman had he, nor more servants, no,
At that time, for he chose to travel so;
And he was clad in coat and hood of green.
A sheaf of peacock arrows bright and keen
Under his belt he bore right carefully
(Well could he keep his tackle yeomanly:
His arrows had no draggled feathers low),
And in his hand he bore a mighty bow.
A cropped head had he and a sun-browned face.
Of woodcraft knew he all the useful ways.
Upon his arm he bore a bracer gay,
And at one side a sword and buckler, yea,
And at the other side a dagger bright,
Well sheathed and sharp as spear point in the light;
On breast a Christopher of silver sheen.
He bore a horn in baldric all of green;
A forester he truly was, I guess."

—From The Canon's Yeoman's Tale, Canterbury
Tales, Geoffrey Chaucer, Late 14th Century

Bushcraft and prepping are both modern words, new terms for old subjects – survivalism, backwoodsmanship, yeomanry, homesteading, small holding, peasantry... I worry when I read comments on forums that many people have fear and paranoia as the basis for their entry into this community. It is essential to be aware of how the world is changing, and to be prepared for possible future events, but to live in fear is anathema to prepping.

Prepping should instil confidence. It's an insurance for a continuity of lifestyle. When others are wasting their money and time on televisions and gadgets and fads and fashions, the prepping and bushcraft community is learning skills for the future.

While it is essential to stock up on basic and luxury items which will become scarce, even in regional flooding or a hurricane strike, never mind a complete end of the world as we know it situation, these should not be the primary focus.

> *"Only by taking responsibility for oneself, to the greatest extent possible, can one ever be free, and only a free person can make responsible choices - between right and wrong, saving and spending, giving or taking."*

—Paul Ryan

The Tao of Prepping is about changing your mindset, about thinking about how you live, and questioning if it's really good. Is your lifestyle healthy? Is it sustainable? Being completely reliant on supermarket products cannot be good. If the supermarket closes, if there is disruption to the transport chain, what will your children eat? What will you eat? Being completely reliant on money and credit, what will you do when they switch off the ATMs? What will you do when they call in your loan? What will you do when you lose your job and can't pay your mortgage?

It's at these times, usually too late, that people begin to question if they really needed higher purchase for that new flat screen TV, if they really needed to trade in their two year old car for a shinier, newer model. These are just gimmicks. We have been hypnotized into toiling and slaving in order to buy crap which keeps us poor, which makes us slaves. Prepping and bushcraft should be about removing ourselves from that vicious, endless cycle, to a greater or lesser extent. The ultimate dream of many is to become totally self-sufficient but, for the majority, this will remain but a dream. You must pay tax. If you don't pay tax you face the law. You still have to buy the solar panels and the batteries. Unless you're importing sugar yourself, you have to buy it.

> *"Who controls the food supply controls the people. Who controls the energy can control whole continents; who controls the money can control the world."*
>
> —Henry Kissinger

But you can become partially self-sufficient and self-reliant simply by rejecting much of what we're told on TV and in the media. The best thing you could do, for you and your family, is get rid of your television. Just get rid of it. It really, truly isn't necessary and if you knew anything about binaural frequencies it would give you the chills. All it does is fill your head with fear, lies, fantasies, longing and envy. It's parasitic. At best, it just wastes your time.

We, as humans, only live for about seventy years. How mu

eing herded like cattle and then packed like sardines, slowly roasted in the sun, kept in tiny rooms or on plastic lilos. Instead of wasting such money, take your family into the country. Get a tent and go camping, go walking. Start learning new skills.

"Learning is not compulsory... neither is survival"

—W. Edwards Deming

If you find yourself having to hire a plumber or an electrician or a welder, or you need some building work done, then take a course at night school. Learn how to do things yourself. The most valuable people after a global cataclysm will be the ones this generation has lost. For some reason, the skilled working class has all but disappeared. It's no longer fashionable. Everyone wants to work in an office pushing paper or electronic data from one office to the next, pressing buttons on a computer. It's no longer *in* to be a mechanic, but it is exactly these skills – the carpenter, the metal worker, the roof layer – which will be most in demand; these will be the people who can move from community to community and always have a full belly. The same goes for the nurse, the doctor, the dentist, the veterinarian, the tree surgeon, the farmer, the gamekeeper and the soldier.

People will beg them to help.

No-one will need their accounts doing, no-one will need to file insurance claims. Even if you do work in an office environment, start learning manual skills, not just for the end of the world, but for your own mental and financial well-being.

We, as humans, are not designed to sit in one place. The education system is what trains us for this. This is why we spend so many years in school, seated at desks having to stand up or sit down when someone in authority enters the room, fearing grades and report cards. It isn't in any way natural. It is purely to prepare us for a monotonous, mind-wiping career in an office, a cubicle existence, so that we can all buy the products that are flashed in front of our eyes.

Step out of this. Meet people with similar interests. Even if you don't like each other's personalities and characters, learn to appreciate people for what they know and what they can do. We're not plastic, we're not Barbie and Ken. We're told we should be like clones, that we should only like pretty people, or people with expensive clothing or with big cars. In what way would that help you? It's far better to know someone who when they make a pie at home they think of you and bring you one also, than someone who can tell you how much their golf club membership cost. For that you feel small and insignificant.

Do sports which not only train your body and mind but also have future purpose and use. Push yourself.

Do archery, try climbing and canoeing, maybe even potholing or horse riding, certainly rambling or cycling. Don't shy away from new energetic activities now as you may be forced to do them with no practice or training when disaster strikes. Rather than go to the gym, chop wood, dig, fell run, then you will develop muscles which have a purpose rather than those which are purely fashionable. You may not look like Schwarzenegger or Heidi Klum but it will keep you healthy and you will develop real muscles.

> *"A declining institution often experiences survival of the unfittest"*

—John McCarthy

Walk, don't drive. Start walking everywhere; there's no reason not to. If you can, walk to work, go on walking holidays; the more time you spend walking, the better for you. The human body is designed for it. We're not designed to run fast as our knees are on backwards; we're not designed to cycle as we weren't born with wheels – we're designed to walk very long distances. Sedentary lifestyle is what causes obesity and, ultimately, heart disease and death. Post SHTF, the obese and unfit won't last very long... Start getting cardiovascular now.

Addictions

"Whether you sniff it, smoke it, eat it, or shove it up your ass, the result is the same: addiction"

—William Burroughs

"Moderation is the secret of survival."

—Manly Hall

Humans have the ability to become addicted to different things very quickly. Some of us are addicted to tobacco, some alcohol, others drugs, some of us computer games or the Internet and social networking sites, some of us are addicted to adrenalin sports, some to caffeine or chocolate; a diverse range. What's really important is that you learn about yourself.

The Greeks had a phrase – *Gnothi Seuton* – Know Thyself. In the modern world we're told to only look at the good things, to promote our better side. We've all done this when applying for jobs, we don't tell them about our weaknesses, our little flaws, our bad traits. But we all have them.

Preparing for future survival, and living well now, entails dissecting ourselves, learning about what's good about us and what's bad. Addictions are the most extreme form of bad artificial personality traits. Some of us may be bitter, or jealous, or resentful or angry or lazy and these aspects can be very hard to overcome as they're ingrained in our characters. However, you weren't born addicted to coffee or cigarettes, nor are they from childhood trauma of the Freudian kind.

The major problem with addictions, for preppers, is that many of the things we're addicted to are luxury items, and will become extremely scarce should problems arise in the future. There are many different ways around this, rehab being one; some preppers stock up on chocolate, thousands of chocolate bars stored away in case of emergency. But what happens if the house is destroyed? An earthquake or a tornado means they won't have access to this precious stock. Wouldn't it be better to remove the addiction rather than stocking up for it?

Tobacco is smoked mostly in the form of cigarettes, and these come nicely pre-made, pre-rolled, pre-packaged, contain over 5000 unknown chemicals and are very expensive. Smoking is an extremely expensive and dangerous habit. I smoked cigarettes for 25 years. My children kept asking me to stop, so I did, about eight months ago. But I discovered that

I can't live without nicotine, at least not pleasantly. I tried going cold turkey but I just couldn't manage. So I smoke a pipe. I use raw tobacco and smoke that, sometimes flavoured with vanilla. And the great thing about tobacco is that you can grow it yourself. The seeds are tiny; one fingertip can hold thousands of them. They're smaller than poppy seeds. However, it's no alternative in taste or quality to brand name products. Gandalf had a specific reason why he visited the Shire... The fact remains, though, that we can grow it ourselves, and this is very important. I also save money by not buying from corporations, a huge amount of money comparatively speaking, and that money can go on more essential goods for my family – food, clothing, paying bills.

Alcohol is probably the worst drug there is. Forget crack and smack; alcohol destroys more families than all other drugs combined. And it's perfectly legal. And it's expensive. And it turns intelligent, witty, sane people into utter arseheads. One of the first addictions which must be overcome is alcohol, especially alcohol which has been produced by corporations. It bears little semblance to the healthier, home grown stuff.

If you like beer, learn to make your own. Even if you live in a flat you can make your own. It's cheap, it's healthy and you know exactly what goes in it. The same goes for wine, make your own. You don't need to impress people with the vintage of a store-bought Chablis; that tells nothing about you, more about how quickly you like to throw money away. If you really want to impress people, practice and practice until you can make an excellent elderflower champagne. These are skills which will be needed and, at the same time, will help you today. They will save you money and it will mean you're not addicted to a corporate product sold in plastic pubs at extortionate prices.

If you're addicted to the more exotic drugs, whether of the illegal or prescription varieties, then I can only suggest you stop. There is no benefit. Don't convince yourself otherwise. There are many natural alternatives which grow wild in our own woodlands and fields, or which can be easily grown domestically, but I'll speak no more on that subject...

Social networking sites destroy families and destroy relationships. They also enable corporations, advertising agencies and governments, both domestic and foreign, to monitor your every single move, and also your friends'. Just log off. Do you really need to chat with someone you knew twenty years ago, or discover what they thought of the last pizza they ate? If you really need to talk with someone, do so face-to-face, go have tea with them, don't just sit there tapping at a screen.

I've seen many preppers preparing, bizarrely and paradoxically, for a TEOTWAWKI situation where they can recharge their mobile phones, and there are many products on the market just for this. While the mobile is an excellent invention, it has completely removed privacy and it is highly unlikely that after a global disaster mobile networks will still have coverage. Learn to be without your mobile. It's another addiction. Go away for the weekend and leave it at home.   When I was young, we had a land-line and I remember quite distinctly that we didn't take it camping with us, nor did we need it. If you're going hillwalking, then yes, it is useful for calling the emergency services but there are simpler alternatives and you are less likely to ruin the short time you have in the wilds by being worried about someone calling you or not.

Basically, anything artificial which you really don't need but feel you are dependent on you need to get rid of, or find a healthier home-made alternative which you can use both now and after a major disaster. Coffee, for example. Dandelion roots can make an excellent coffee substitute. They don't contain caffeine and taste more like chicory but after a few weeks of drinking it you won't notice. Your body does not need caffeine.

Sugar. Stop eating sugar. Stop using sugared products. If you really need something sweet, go to a bee-keeper and buy genuine honey (not the fake artificially-flavoured corn syrup stuff sold in supermarkets), or eat fruit. If you're ambitious and have enough land, try keeping bees yourself.

Use honey sparingly as a treat, as was done throughout human history. It's a luxury item. Kept as a special treat you will appreciate the taste far, far more; it will be like an exquisite elixir, unlike the spoonfuls of white, bleached cane sugar shoved into every cup of tea. And as for tea, there are a myriad of herbs and fruits which you can forage or grow and make your own. If you're feeling stressed at the end of the day, and you want to sleep, have some lemon balm. It's easy to grow. With just a few leaves you'll feel relaxed. And don't buy tea in packets. There's absolutely no need. It's a waste of money and a con. You don't need to fund corporations or slave labour in third world countries, you can do it yourself. Get a book on teas or herbs, read up on what you really need. You need one for energy, maybe one for colds and coughs, you need one for sleeping, for stress, things like that, and then grow them in little pots on your windowsill or pick them out in the bush.

There are so many things you can do for yourself, firstly to remove an addiction, and secondly to stop paying out and therefore increase the quality of your present lifestyle. Save money. You work hard for your money, why throw it away just because an advertising agency has told you that if you buy X then you'll feel like a superstar, or a model, or a famous actor, or a sports personality, or a 1970s surfer? Don't fall deeper into the trap. Get out of it now.

Prepping is not just about the end of the world, it's about becoming more and more self-reliant. There are so many things you can do, and so many ways to do them.

I walked back down the hill, still in the blistering heat. The wind howled and whispered. I had to walk through and around an immense herd of white cattle tended by two gypsies seated in the shade of some hawthorns. They asked me, ironically, if I'd been mushroom hunting. I said no. They commented on the heat and I laughed, then walked on.

In the valley below, the two red onion dome spires of the village church stood prominent against the backdrop of green. Horseflies continued to buzz about me, brought in their hordes by the cows. They sought out weak spots in my sopping cloth armour.

Every day is an adventure, but it doesn't matter where you live. It is important to look for the beauty and to feel at peace with your surroundings, wherever that may be. However, there are settings which are poisonous to Man. If you can see only concrete and brickwork, pylons and no greenery, no wildlife, then you're in the wrong place. It doesn't matter how but find a way to relocate, even if the greenery is but a tiny plot where a few insects crawl and the occasional bird swoops down to peck them off; it is still a place where you can allow your mind to filter back into the earth and feel at one with it. When we surround ourselves with concrete and electronics, in the digital world, we enter another plane of existence, one which is not our own. It's an artificial construct. The wool has been pulled over our eyes. We don't belong there. We are fish out of water and therefore more easily manipulated.

> *"You begin saving the world by saving one man at a time; all else is grandiose romanticism or politics"*

—Charles Bukowski

The more self-reliant we are, the stronger our wills become, and the harder to control by external forces without our best interests at heart. Prepping and bushcraft are about taking back that control, and putting it back into our own hands; not just for when disaster happens, but of immediate effect. It's not a revolution against a government or a country or anybody else. It's a personal revolution. It's a revolution which says "This is me, this is my family, this is where I want to be and what I want to do, I will make my own decisions about what I eat, what I wear, with whom I speak, and where I walk..."

Tao of Prepping

The Lost Generation

"Thousands of tired, nerve-shaken, over-civilized people are beginning to find out going to the mountains is going home; that wilderness is a necessity..."

—John Muir

"This generation has given up on growth. They're just hoping for survival."

—Penelope Spheeris

Whilst many preppers and bushcrafters and homesteaders get into this field because of various concerns about the future, or because of past experience, many are what could be termed the Lost Generation. The modern world has left them deluded, disillusioned, disappointed, disenfranchised; they don't fit in. There's something wrong with it. Many are the progeny of the hippy generation, or 1970s rebellion. Some grew up in the 1990s, after the fall of the 1980's western materialist capitalist credit bubble, until that collapsed and people began tightening their belts again and not re-mortgaging to take that second holiday in the sun.

There seems to be a great longing among many to return to a more simple, natural way of life, the ideal being having a homestead or smallholding, growing your own crops, tending your own livestock, making your own clothes and furniture, hunting for game, the life of the original American frontiersman and woman. But, for the vast majority, this has become an impossibility.

The price of land is at an all time high and is owned in swathes by a tiny few. Forest belongs to trusts and corporations and is no longer the native deciduous, instead merely quick-growing farmed coniferous, which means nothing lives within it. The cost of buying a small cottage with a little plot of land is beyond the capability of most and is but a dream when many struggle to put food on their plates day by day, when jobs are no longer for life and now earn minimum wage.

There is also something more primal missing. It's a sense which our ancestors felt which we desperately want to feel again. It's the same sense you get when you sit by an open campfire at night, poking a stick into the embers. It's that connection to nature, the connection to our more primal selves where we had to rely on our own skills and merit. I am Man, I am Woman.

> *"The only hope is that our civilization will collapse at a certain point, as always happens in history. Then, out of barbarity, a renaissance. "*

—Pierre Schaeffer

Our natural, primal essence has been stripped away from us, and other labels have been tacked onto our now plastic selves. So there are many who, whilst preparing for future disasters or cataclysms, are also secretly hoping that it's a chance for us all to start again. They're hoping that those powers that be who dictate every aspect of our lives, and leave most of us as little more than slaves, will suddenly have their power stripped from them, that the electricity will go off, the lights will go out, the oil will run dry, and that the vast majority who live for their hero of the week, from singing or dancing or skating programmes, will be stuck starving at closed supermarkets, begging at abandoned and sealed banks, fighting amongst one another for the last morsels of packaged food, imported and genetically modified, and sold under home brands by megachains with fluorescent lighting and Muzak spilling down the aisles.

Those preppers and bushcrafters hope that if they just sit and ride out the storm for one week, two weeks, perhaps a month, then this gross population of *sheeple* will have diminished to such a level that society will be unable to kick-start itself back into motion again. And that they, and they alone, will be the founders of the New World Order; healthier, stronger, more nature-based, more like our ancestors held dear, than what advertisers promote.

There are some who are utter fantasists who long for the peculiar – alien invasions, zombie apocalypse – and they prepare themselves accordingly with bizarre weaponry and vehicles but, for the majority, for those that hope that at some point the current societal nightmare will end, they try to learn and stock up and hope that their day will come, and that they will get their chance to shine.

Community

"One of the most destructive things that's happening in modern society is that we are losing our sense of the bonds that bind people together - which can lead to nightmares of social collapse."

—Alexander McCall Smith

"No man is an island"

—John Donne

The Hollywoodesque image of the lone mountain man is little more than a fantasy. There is a tiny number of people capable of going out to the bush and living indefinitely on their own merit. We, as humans, are a communal species. We rely on one another, not just for skills which individual members may lack, but for companionship and conversation. When we have a problem we like to discuss it. When we have worries we like to have a second opinion. When we have dreams, fantasies, ambitions, we like to share.

We need friendship. More importantly, we need family.

The modern world has stripped away the notion of family and made us all individuals. It's removed the idea of home and instead sold the idea of *cribs*. By isolating people from the basic nuclear structure that is the foundation of society it makes them more dependable on larger bodies such as the State, world organizations, and corporations. When you have a family, when you have a close group of friends, you don't automatically turn to some government body for help; you ask your friends or family first and, in turn, when they need help they ask you. So it is with prepping.

While there is a temptation to go out and get every latest piece of kit, if you have a family you must then buy the same kit for each member. Thinking on this individualistic wave length, the anti-tribe, is what has been drummed into us since childhood through the media and through education. Instead of thinking about buying for yourself, think about buying for a group.

If you've ever had to feed fifteen or twenty people then you'll know that the last thing you would look for would be a mess tin, you'd be looking for a Dutch oven or cauldron. If you've ever needed to house fifteen or twenty people then you'll know that the last thing you'd be looking for would be an expensive micro-lite hammock with tarpaulin and mosquito net, instead you'd be looking for a patrol tent or even a marquee. The same goes for food. Buying microwaveable gourmet meals is fine if there is just one or two of you, but when feeding the five thousand you need large stocks of raw produce. Buying in bulk is always cheaper; growing your own is even cheaper still.

> *"Through the evolutionary process, those who are able to engage in social cooperation of various sorts do better in survival and reproduction."*
>
> —Robert Nozick

If you have a community then you can share tasks. If one is cooking, then one is preparing and another is peeling and chopping. Do the jobs together and not only do you do them quicker but you also spend time with one another and bond. Friendships are based on experiencing both good and bad times together, they're not based solely on a shared interest on the Internet.

Until you've really spent time with someone, and got to know them closely and personally, then they're not real, they're abstract, and they can be instantly disposed of with the click of a button. But when you've been through hardships together, when you've cried and laughed together, a bond is formed. The longer you spend with a person or with a group, the more you get to know who you can trust, who you can rely on, and who you can't. This is essential not just for the future but also for the now. The better you know your closer circle, the bigger your close circle is, the less likely you are to rely on handouts from bureaucratic bodies who want your soul in return.

Traditionally, the root of all society is the family – a mother, a father, children, grandparents, cousins, aunts, uncles and so on. The family is the single most important facet of our lives. Without family, we are lost, wandering individuals, and very few of us can survive on our own, either financially or psychologically. We, as humans, need a home. We need a mother to feed us and care for us; we need a father to provide for us and to teach us those skills we will need in life. We need siblings for support. We need people we can trust and no friend can ever replace the biological link we have to our own flesh and blood.

Blood is blood.

Our parents raise us and provide for us when we are young, they give us the grounding we need to stand on our own two feet. As we get older and have children of our own, our parents – now as grandparents and retired – should be there to look after our infants so that we can work and provide for the family, for both the old and the young. When our children age and our parents reach the point where they can no longer sustain themselves, then it is our turn to look after our parents.

Old people should not be sent to some private nursing home to be looked after and which costs a ridiculous amount of money; nor should our children be put in expensive day-care – we can solve both problems by living together. Both should be tended to at home. The elderly looked after us, we look after them. As we age and our children have children then the wheel turns and it is our turn to look after our grandchildren and, when we become frail and old, our children will look after us.

Many countries, especially around the Mediterranean, see all family members in three generations living under one roof, with each generation helping the next. That is how family should be. That is how family has been since the dawn of time – not this insane dysfunctional farce disguised as political correctness which is being forced down our throats nowadays; a farce which has destroyed the bedrock of society and turned us all into government-dependent parasites.

The family which supports itself and each member grows rich and strong and powerful. The family which separates and divides fails, leaving its children lost. A broken home is a broken home, regardless of what political spin is put on it. What is the burning desire to leave home and to go into debt to rent a flat or bedsit, or take a mortgage on a house which will chain us to banks for the rest of our lives? If a family works together and stays together then each member can live at home – with tolerance and respect – and the entire family can live well and free.

A community is a collection of families, all living side by side, all supporting one another. A community is not a collection of broken homes and broken families – that's just chaos and crime as there is no central root.

Forget political correctness and the new fashions pounded into our heads by media and government propaganda. Family is everything. Think about your actions and act responsibly as what you do now affects not just our generation but every generation to come – what we do now creates the future.

Clan is a word which fits the prepping and bushcraft community very well. While there are some attempts being made to unite this community on a national, and even international, scale (P2S being the most successful in the UK), ultimately at the base level it comes down to clans – people who live within a localized geographic area, preferably within walking distance, as these are the people who you will turn to first when the lights go out and the oil runs dry. However, and more importantly, these are the people you can turn to now, long before that ever happens. If you can't rely on them now then forget relying on them when the SHTF as they will have already shown their mettle.

Prepping is about changing your mindset now, living now how you want to live in the future.

While there are some legal restrictions – you can't walk around with a Bowie knife and you can't camp where you like – you can do other other things which change how you fit into society and, when more people begin growing their own food and stop buying resource-heavy imported foods at the wrong time of the year, or running gas guzzling engines, or buying the latest products from computer corporations every time there's a new tweek, then perhaps society will begin to change in general.

> *"All truth passes through three stages. First, it is ridiculed. Second, it is violently opposed. Third, it is accepted as being self-evident"*
>
> —Arthur Schopenhauer

It is better to be the avante garde than the masses following, even if that avante garde is at first ridiculed by TPTB and the sheeple, content to be told how to live their own lives, and that everything is fine and dandy, nothing to see here, please move on, instead of questioning and working it out for themselves.

The Kill

> "In our struggle to restrain the violence and contain the damage, we tend to forget that the human capacity for aggression is more than a monstrous defect, that it is also a crucial survival tool. "

—Katherine Dunn

> "Hunting is not a sport. In a sport, both sides should know they're in the game."

—Paul Rodriguez

There is something genetically inherent in all of us, regardless of what philosophy we may have acquired in life, that predisposes us to hunt, to kill and to eat animals. There is something

Tao of Prepping

intangible, an adrenaline rush, a sense of pride; it's primal, from our reptilian brains. It's part of our carnivorous nature. While many are vegetarians, they would find themselves facing a very difficult philosophical decision in an environment where they could not sustain themselves, or their family, merely by foraging alone and where game was plentiful. However, there is something wrong, incredibly wrong, about hunting when there is no need to do so. It is far better to learn how to track and observe an animal and let it live than to slay it merely because the opportunity arises.

People often expect to be treated as something special because they have managed to kill an animal. If I met someone who could bring an animal back from the dead then I would be impressed. Anyone can kill. Usually, it relies on luck, opportunity and determination, with a tiny smattering of skill involved.

As preppers and bushcrafters and homesteaders, hunting, killing, and preparing game is a major factor in our make-up. These are skills we have to know. These separate the self-reliant from the supermarket dependent.

Anyone who has ever raised their own chicken or rabbit, fed it daily, tended it, cured its illnesses, and then killed it, plucked it, skinned it, gutted it, butchered it, cooked it and then eaten it, will tell you that it's a completely different experience than just buying a pre-packaged frozen, bleached carcass.

It is the balance of this which the prepper must deeply meditate upon, and the balance is to do with necessity.

Do you really need that animal to be dead?

Are you in such dire circumstances that you cannot live without consuming it? Without its flesh, or its hide or its horn? The answer, in the modern world, 99% of the time, is no.

So why do it?

The first necessity is to learn *how* to do it. Most of prepping in the modern world requires learning the skills that can be used after a cataclysm because without learning through experience you may not have the opportunity to practice and try again when your life depends on it. So it is better to do things now when you have a home, than to wait until later when you may not.

Snake skin being scrubbed clean with salt

In this case, each should learn how to track, how to hunt, how to humanely bring down game, how to butcher it and prepare it, skin it and cure and tan, under expert guidance and supervision – not through trial and error, because that would be inhumane. And once you have learned those skills, hopefully on the first occasion, then store that knowledge and keep it safe somewhere at the back of your mind until you really need it.

Some people develop a lust for the kill, and get into the sporting side. This has no logic whatsoever. It's not sporting – it's slaughter. You're not competing against the animal – try hunting on the African Savannah with nothing but a loin cloth and a pointed stick and that would be sporting. Hunting for sport removes you so far from the natural cycle of things. No tribe has ever gone out and slaughtered game for fun, because when you do that you deplete next year's stocks and next year you discover that there aren't enough animals to feed you and then you starve and then die.

Animals, even wild game, must be tended like a crop. You only take those which are weak or old, or in surplus. And each time you take a life you must thank it. You must thank the spirit of that creature for providing you and your family with food. It died for you. You better be grateful.

Homesteaders, on the other hand, are in a different situation. To be completely self-reliant requires raising your own livestock and that, ultimately, requires you slaughtering it for food. Most of us are meat eaters but the meat we eat comes from the most disgusting factories you can imagine, where animals are poorly treated, crammed together, fed antibiotics and growth hormones and the remains of other animals, and are slaughtered well before the correct traditional age, merely so that the company can make higher profits. In that case, the homesteader is correct. They raise the animal with love and care, feed it and, when it comes time for the slaughter, it is dispatched humanely after having lived quite a decent life. And the cycle continues.

There is something spiritual about raising your own livestock and consuming it, but only if you are humane and logical, and don't bend to corporate pressure and profit at the sake of the animals' welfare. It would be good if all preppers, bushcrafters and homesteaders simply stopped buying meat from supermarkets and butchers. Buy from a local farm, buy from other homesteaders who raise their own. Buy from places where you can see how the animals are reared. The meat will be more expensive but we don't need to eat meat every day of the week. Don't buy from anonymous sources in far flung countries.

Unlike growing your own veg, raising any form of livestock is a major commitment. Having the space and time to do it prevents most from starting. And this is a very good thing. Unless you've spent time working on a farm or have other first-hand, long-term experience with raising animals for food then don't do it until you have. Rearing animals under poor conditions, even if your intent is good, is wrong and, in many cases, illegal. If you really want to try your hand at it then go learn from experts. Even a goat needs milking twice a day, at dawn and dusk, every day, for the rest of its life – are you seriously able or willing to make such a commitment? Forget holidays and camping trips unless you can find someone to stand-in for you.

Only buy leather goods when you know the cow or the goat which provided it was reared in a humane manner, not as in China where many cows are stripped of their skin whilst still alive, prior to being dispatched; where the skin is ripped from its body by a machine and the cow screams in agony as it goes along the conveyor belt before it has a bolt put through its skull, or is electrocuted. And then its meat is utterly tainted beyond comprehension by adrenaline and fear, and that is what you tuck into when you order steak. Far better that an animal had pasture and good hay and was cared for before being dispatched humanely and then butchered.

The same goes for fish. Never buy fish in a tin. Chances are that it's not the fish you think you're buying because global stocks have been greatly depleted and alternatives are being used, especially in the case of tuna, salmon and cod. Do you really need fish that badly? If so, get yourself a fishing rod and learn how to fish and then catch your own.

Stop seeing animals, fish and birds as merely another product. I laughed when I discovered that the new term for personnel is human resources. We too, as humans, are slowly becoming little more than numbered products. Don't see animals, birds and fish in the same way. They have lives, they have spirits. When you consume them, you are consuming their spirit. Thank them for that and imagine where were they raised, and on what, because whatever they were fed on you are putting into your own body, and one of the greatest needs for the prepper is to cleanse their bodies from the poisons and pharmaceuticals that corporations have infected us with, and which have destroyed our immune systems, our children's immune systems, and have led to insane diseases and mass culling among livestock. Yet most of us continue to eat this poisoned, uncared-for flesh.

> *"To cherish what remains of the Earth and to foster its renewal is our only legitimate hope of survival."*

> —Wendell Berry

Respect nature. Enjoy wildlife in the wild. Learn how to hunt, and how to do it properly, and then sit back and let nature take its course. Help bring down corporate farms and factories by not buying from them. When corporations learn that they're not making a profit, they'll pull out of that industry.

Don't use fast food chains which use unidentifiable meat by-products. You know the ones. Do you really think that they're free range cattle which fill those burgers? Or free range hens in that deep fried bucket? We have no idea what's inside them. Horse and donkey, and pink slime, for starters.

Begin eating only that which you know and can identify, and which you can be absolutely sure of. Protect your own well being and, by doing so, you'll protect the well-being of the creatures that you consume.

The Smoke House

"To retain respect for sausages and laws, one must not watch them in the making."

—Otto von Bismarck

Modern cooking relies on two devices, neither of which would function – or even have a practical counterpart – should we lose electricity: the microwave and the fridge-freezer. The traditional means of preserving meat for the Ruthenians where I live is to smoke it. This both cooks the meat and prolongs its usability.

There are two methods for smoking meat – hot smoking and cold smoking. Unless you intend to eat the hot smoked meat within a couple of days it is always better to cold smoke it. However, hot smoking does have its uses, as shall be seen...

Many village houses here build their smoke house out of an old metal locker – the type found in changing rooms around the world. Metal is an ideal material as it won't catch fire, although you must make sure to remove all paint from both inside and outside the locker prior to smoking or you might end up poisoning your food. Some villagers build their smoke house from the ground up using bricks and a wooden plank chamber on top. For my own smoke house I chose to use a solid wood cupboard – don't use MDF as it will warp, plus it contains toxic glue.

I found an old cupboard (6' x 2' x 2') inside my log garden house and, after much exertion, managed to get it into the garden. I chose to stand it in an area where, should it catch fire, it would be unlikely to ignite anything else – wood shed, roof, etc. Note that during the smoking process, the smoke house will get incredibly hot, too hot to touch.

I laid the cupboard on its back and chainsawed out the floor. Watch out for hidden nails. I didn't and had to have my entire chain resharpened before I could use it again.   Next, I knocked out the top shelf but left the wooden clothes rail in place. This would be used to hang the meat from. If your cupboard or locker doesn't have one then you'll have to install a rod yourself.

The interior of the cupboard was filled with cobwebs and mouse droppings so I brushed those out and then prepared to do a hot smoke simply to purify the inside of the cupboard – the heat and smoke would kill off any germs, insects or any other nasty I'd missed. I stood the cupboard up and placed a metal bucket in the centre of the, now earthen, floor. I lit a small fire inside using paper and kindling and, when it was hot enough, placed some alder wood on to provide the smoke.

Alder-wood is the basic material you'll need for all smoking as it doesn't really burn but instead smoulders, producing thick acrid smoke – which is why you should never use it in your fireplace or for cooking. Elder is a weed which grows incredibly rapidly and will return year upon year so you should never run out. Elder will also regrow from a cut log. There are a lot of superstitions surrounding Elder and early European peoples believed older trees contained powerful female spirits which should be placated before chopping down their home.

I closed the door to the smoke house and let the smoking begin. Two important additions you'll need to add to your door are some form of lock – a simple wooden block to keep the door shut – because when the cupboard gets hot the sides and door will warp and the door will pop open, losing your smoke; also, a heat-proof handle. I find that a coiled strap of thick leather nailed to the door does the trick – whatever you do, don't use a metal handle or you'll be leaving your skin on it.

After several hours the smoke will begin seeping through cracks and from in between the planks. If you use a metal locker it will come through the vents. Don't worry about this as you need a tiny amount of airflow to keep the fire smouldering.

As the main object of using a smoke house is to preserve meat for months, it's necessary to next convert it into a cold smoker. To do this, I moved the cupboard to where it would be placed permanently, and raised it on bricks. I laid the bricks flat so they ran the entire circumference of the bottom of the cupboard and left a gap in the front. Next, I piled earth around the bricks making them airtight. Then, I dug a small trench, 6 inches deep by four inches wide, running 4 feet away from the smoke house. At the end of this trench, I widened out the hole for a fire-pit to 8 inches wide by 8 inches long by 8 inches deep.

Next, I used a 4" diameter metal concertina-like chimney flue (very flexible) and fed one end in between the gap in the bricks and then upwards, so that it opened up, perhaps 2 inches above the ground, into the smoke house. The rest of the flue I laid out at the bottom of the trench so that it ended at the beginning of the fire-pit, a couple of inches above it. I then filled in the trench with soil and patted it down, and filled any gap between the flue and the bricks, making it all air tight.

You'll need to find a big flat stone to cover half the fire-pit with, and it's also a good idea to place flat stones over the length of the flattened earth above the flue to distribute the weight if you accidentally stand on that area.

Basically, the principle is as follows – you light a small fire in the fire-pit (the further away from the smoke house the better), and, when it's hot enough, load it with alder for smoke and apple-wood for flavour. Any fruit tree will work, and each has its own unique taste. With the fire-pit half covered by a stone roof, air will enter and blow the smoke back along the pipe to the smoke house. It's called cold smoking because as the smoke travels along the pipe its heat dissipates into the soil – the colder the smoke that reaches the smoke-house, the longer the meat will last. If you hot smoke your meat (fire inside the smoke-house) or if the flue is too short, you'll end up cooking the meat and it will go bad quickly, same as if you'd cooked it in an oven. Hot smoking is usually only done to add a smoky flavour, not to preserve.

Once the fire is producing a decent and steady flow of smoke, you can hang your meat from the rod. The longer, and colder, you smoke the meat, the longer it will last. I've smoked sausages for 12 hours and they've lasted 3 months. Many people smoke for 24 hours and sausages will last for 6 months when stored in a dry place.

Remember to keep stocking the fire – don't let it go out. The aim is to starve the meat of oxygen and dry it out. The best thing about building a smoke house is that it makes superb foodstuffs and you can use it again and again. Once you've made your own home-made sausages you'll never want to eat store-bought ones again.

Tao of Prepping

Sewerage

"The grass is always greener over the septic tank"

—Erma Bombeck

There are many aspects of civilization which either go unnoticed or which are left unmentioned but, without which, society would collapse. One of these is sewerage.

The simple act of being able to go to the toilet and flush away waste bodily products to places unseen is a crowning feature of the modern world – it has drastically reduced disease and infection. Should there be a point where toilets stop flushing or water gets disconnected, most people don't realize just how much bodily waste the average family produces per day – and they certainly haven't considered what to do with it.

Resorting to the medieval method of dumping the pan into the street would quickly lead to epidemics so alternative methods must be employed. The locals in my area rely on one of two simple methods to dispose of waste – either an outhouse or a septic tank.

Many of the older generation prefer the outhouse because it doesn't cost anything to run. Each garden has a wooden thunder-box with a wooden tray two feet beneath the seat. After every couple of uses, some sawdust or sand is thrown on the tray's contents, and the tray is used until it is filled. At this point, you simply dig a hole somewhere and empty the contents into it, fill in the hole with soil and reuse the tray. Some people even grow trees on top of the filled-in holes to benefit from the manure and also to prevent people accidentally stepping on the mound.

The second method, and the one I personally use, is the septic tank. Having this system means you can have the luxury of an indoor toilet (no going out at night with a torch in the freezing cold). As with a modern system, the toilet has a pipe leading outside which carries away the waste but, unlike a modern system which leads into a large sewage disposal network, the pipe ends in a septic tank at the bottom of the garden.

Some septic tanks can cost a lot of money and are made of metal or plastic. Mine was an old concrete pipe about 4 feet across and ten feet deep, covered by a hand made iron cover (which doesn't fit too well). The hole into which the pipe was placed was dug by hand. Gravity takes the waste from the toilet to the septic tank after each flush as the pipe runs downhill and emerges into the concrete pipe at about one foot beneath the cover.

The downside of having a septic tank is that it must be emptied regularly. Groundwater can seep in, especially after heavy rain, and fill it. The locals usually leave the bottom of the tank unsealed so that water can filter back into the ground but this also works negatively after spring thaw or autumn storms. The best method to empty the tank is by using a pump with a long hose pipe ending in a field. If this isn't an option then I'd recommend going with a trusty old thunder-box as the tray's contents can be bagged and carried some distance before being buried.

Heating and Cooking

"People love chopping wood. In this activity one immediately sees results."

—Albert Einstein

Due to the entire region being covered in forest, it is of little surprise that the local Ruthenians use wood for their primary fuel source. In fact, wood plays a major part in the yearly cycle of the locals, as the gathering, preparing, storing and use of timber is a never ending process and often requires the villagers to work in groups to get a job done.

The above picture shows a traditional 'pec' oven, along with a Babka bed in a kitchen. Note the multiple doors and drawers for stocking the fire, baking, bread making, etc. A pec can be built by hand with minimal material and equipment.

When I bought my house, it came with a traditional *pec*, a large ceramic and brick *aga*-type oven with room enough to sit on, in the kitchen and a smaller, taller version between the two downstairs bedrooms. The bathroom had a, somewhat mobile, wood boiler for water, something similar to a *samovar*. The pec was in a fairly sad state and instead of repairing it, I knocked it down and installed a modern glass-fronted fireplace to function as my primary heating source. A bad, bad mistake as I was to find out.

In the kitchen, which was once the cow shed, I installed a modern gas oven and connected a butane cylinder to it as there was no mains gas available in the village at the time. The cylinder-fuelled oven has turned out to be a great success story as it means we can cook in a modern fashion, extremely cheaply – the cylinder only needs changing/refilling twice per year.

But first, back to the fireplace. There is a romantic image of logs crackling and flames roaring in a fireplace while everyone sits around basking in the warmth on cold and frosty evenings. I chose quite a high-powered one, supposedly over 20 kilowatts in power, although I now suspect it is somewhat closer to 10 or 12. We connected it to the old chimney, which had once been the exhaust system for the pec, and then connected a series of metal foil pipes, 4 inches in diameter, to the fireplace. These pipes were then led into the various downstairs rooms, specifically the bedrooms and bathroom, and also upstairs into two of the bedrooms and the hallway. The theory being that hot air would heat throughout the house.

Not so. The simple fact that the house is large and has 2-foot thick stone walls, as well as having old twin glass pane windows, meant that the heat produced by the fireplace was utterly insufficient. There were also large areas not covered by the piping – the kitchen, the dining room, the studio upstairs, as well as the toilet and the master bedroom – and simply having such areas at a constant much lower temperature mean that what little heat was produced quickly dissipated.

I'd also gone for the cheaper option of not having a smoke-free glass front, which meant that after 30 minutes of use the glass blackened and we couldn't even see the fire. I'd also 'opened up' the house by knocking through walls and installing archways. Bad mistake.

There are more modern, and much costlier, methods of heating which we are currently looking into – a wood boiler, installed in the root cellar, connected to radiators looks the best option but deciding between air or water is another issue. Due to the extreme cold during winter here, any water that isn't constantly heated is very likely to freeze, which would mean having to replace radiators or even the entire pipe network in the spring due to frost damage.

Traditionally, the locals used the pec located in the kitchen. These are so large that not only can you cook on the hob, bake bread and heat, but you can also sit on them and play cards. The grandmother of the family, the *Babka*, had her bed in the kitchen next to the pec. Life during winter revolved around the pec and the kitchen as it was the warmest spot in the house. Also, the locals have small, closed off rooms for a purpose – they're easier to trap heat. The small pec in the bedrooms works in a similar fashion but without cooking facilities.

Like an aga, you run the pec on wood or other solid fuels. However, unlike an aga and because of its ceramic outer layer, the pec stays hot long after the fire has died – sometimes for days. Some innovative villagers adapt the ash tray so that its sides form a three-sided pipe. This is then connected to radiators via pipes and the water within is heated continuously by the pec.

Having a three-generation family living in a house means that there is always someone home, usually the Babka, to keep the pec stocked so that it never goes out. For the modern family, without a Babka and with both parents working and kids at school, keeping a fire going is almost impossible which means upon returning home the entire process of cleaning out the ashtray, stocking and lighting must begin again – not fun when there's snow outside and it's dark.Wood is generally collected each year during late summer and early autumn. Many villagers own a parcel of forest but they still have to pay a small fee per cubic metre of logs. Collecting dead-fall gets around this but doesn't compare to the quantity and quality needed. We personally need about 8 or 10 cubic metres per year. A local tractor driver is hired and, with a few men sitting in the trailer, we go off to the forest. A local lumber company will have cut down a designated area and stacked long logs ready for when people come to collect.

Oak and beech are the preferred wood. Much of the new growth is sycamore and birch but they're nowhere near as good for fuel. Pine is never used as it produces little heat and can cause chimney fires.

Always keep an eye out for fresh dead-fall. A recently lightning-struck tree is less likely to be as rotten as one that has lain a while on the forest floor

It's back breaking work hoisting 4 foot long logs, by hand, from the ground onto a trailer until it's filled. The ride back to the village, sitting on the collected logs, is a most enjoyable one.

Once back at the house, the logs are dumped in the garden or yard and a circular saw is set up. It's quite common here, for those without large families to help, to draft in a gang of gypsies, or Roma as they're now called. These Roma will do hard manual work for hours on end and, because they're used to working in family teams, get the job done fairly quickly. It's traditional here to provide food and drink to such work groups, as well as pay them.

The logs are sawn into foot long lengths and for a period of weeks the entire valley rings with the horrific sound of circular saws. An alternative is to use a chainsaw but this works out extremely costly due to petrol consumption. There are several men in the area missing fingers to circular saws as it is exceptionally dangerous work. Once the logs have been shortened, and the Roma gang has moved onto the next house, it's time to chop the wood for seasoning.

Generally, unless the wood is particularly wide of girth, it only needs to be chopped in quarters and then stacked. Sometimes, too many knots mean it remains as a solid log – if it's big enough it can be used as a chopping block.

The best method to quickly chop logs is with an axe – using splitters and wedges is fine if you're dealing with a tiny quantity of wood, but when you're dealing with tons it's easier just to work your way through them swing after swing.

There are three basic sizes of axe – the hatchet, for kindling; the half or boy's axe, and the felling axe. I personally prefer to use a half axe as using a heavy felling axe for hours on end is physically exhausting. Then, there are two different types of axe head – one is for cutting and one is for splitting. At this stage of the wood job a wedge-shaped splitting head is required. Always remember to keep the edge sharp. Sometimes it's necessary to resharpen it several times during the process. Many villagers have a specific maul axe just for log splitting – I prefer to have a multi-purpose one instead.

Axe shafts break. After cleaving away for an extended time your concentration will lower and you'll smash the upper part of the stave against the log or the block. Always keep a spare shaft in store as it is extremely annoying having to stop a day's work in order to go out and buy another – or make

Half axe and hatchet

one. Also, keep a few metal wedges around to secure
the head in place should you need to replace it.
Always make sure that the grain runs length ways
on the shaft – cross-wise grain will fracture quickly.
If the new shaft is too shiny or slippy, rub it over
with coarse grain sand paper – this will give your
hands a better grip.

I'd recommend never buying a metal or plastic
handled axe as the shaft can't be replaced. They look
cool but ultimately you want something which will
last for years.

Once the logs have been chopped it's time to stack
them. Always make sure that the bottom layer is off
the ground otherwise rot will set in. Either use thick
plastic sheeting or build a frame from pallets or
planks. Stack the wood tightly lengthwise with the
bark on top. Cover the whole lot with another plastic
sheet or even a roof if you've got a proper woodshed.
Then leave it for a year.

Long term survival requires long term preparation.
Wood you cut this autumn is for next winter. Using
unseasoned, or wet wood is a waste of wood – it
won't burn properly, nor will it provide the much
needed heat for cooking or heating.

To save doing the same thing day in, day out, prepare your woodpile in three sections. The first section is the logs, which you've already chopped. The next section is the smaller logs to get the fire hot enough so that it can take the bigger ones. For these you can use either the half axe or a hatchet. I prefer to continue using the half axe. Chop the quartered logs in half, then half again. Stack as with the bigger logs, bark side up.

Next comes the kindling. This is what you use to start the fire. One ideal fire-starter is all the sawdust and peelings that were left over from the circular saw. Store these in baskets or even bin bags. Kindling can be anything that's small and burns – next time you take a walk in the wood, gather handfuls of twigs and then store them to dry.

There are disagreements over whether it is better to stack the logs around the house against the wall (as I do) or to have them at a distance in their own woodshed. Having them up against the wall adds to insulation but it is also a fire risk. It's handier for when you need to get more in the night but the wood pile will quickly attract vermin such as mice and insects.

Try not to leave wood too long as it will end up worm-ridden and have the consistency of dust, making it useless for fires. I've learned by making that mistake one too many times.

To start a fire, either in an oven or outside if you're planning on cooking goulash in a cast iron cauldron on a tripod or roasting a rabbit on a spit, you'll need to first set it. Start with balled up newspaper and on top of this place your kindling – twigs or sawdust. On top of that place a few finely chopped pieces of seasoned wood. Then light it. Once the wood starts to burn, add a slightly larger piece. Don't add logs until all the wood is burning. Don't put too much wood on a fire – it isn't necessary and you'll quickly go through your woodpile. One log at a time should do.

The prepping community has over-complicated fire lighting and many of its members have fixated on all manner of unusual tinder to do it. Keep it simple. Unless you're lost up in the mountains then you're likely to have lots of paper knocking about – use that. When you have to light a fire daily for normal living then it loses its 'spark', horrific pun, and instead becomes an unconscious chore.

Tao of Prepping

Water

"Water, water everywhere, nor any drop to drink"

—Samuel Taylor Coleridge

Without water we can last about 3 days so it is one of the four primary concerns for our well-being. For long term living, compared to short term survival, finding a constant fresh and clean water source is of upmost importance. We need water for drinking, cooking and cleaning, as well as a multitude of other tasks.

Many villagers here rely on two basic sources for water – the first is the natural spring. Some springs are 'clean' tasting while others smell like rotten eggs due to their high mineral content. If you're not lucky enough to live near a spring, then the next best thing is to dig a well.

I have observed, on many different occasions, how people discuss water sources, water storage, and filtration systems. Many may not realize that natural springs abound in the wild. Sometimes these are on private land, sometimes on public, but by learning about your local environment, and by taking the time to explore and read up on it, you may begin to map out sources of fresh water. In a cataclysmic situation, where water will become a valuable commodity, as it may do so anyway in the coming years and decades, far surpassing oil as the global conflict instigator, you will be able to remove yourself from the hordes fighting for polluted river water. It means you won't have to stock so much in your house or flat where, ultimately, it will taint from the plastic in which you're storing it.

Investing in a good filtration system, and knowing where nature releases her water, will put you at a far greater advantage than most.

In ancient times, people worshipped wells and springs, and they left gifts for whichever goddess or spirit they believed inhabited it, or perhaps the Mother Goddess herself. Red ribbons were often tied over overhanging branches, perhaps to keep the elves away from poisoning it, or perhaps just as a sign of beauty as a way of saying thanks to the Great Lady who keeps us all alive, yet who we've forgotten and bulldozed over and smeared with concrete. So, if you do find a natural spring far from the madding crowd, take a little gift and bury it nearby, something personal, something thoughtful, and ask the spirit or goddess of the water source to keep providing for you. Thank her for it because when the water runs out, we're all dead.

In our garden there is an old filled-in well. It's a huge affair with round, brick-lined walls, perhaps 4 feet across. This is the simplest method for acquiring groundwater – simply dig a hole deep enough until water begins seeping through the bottom, then shore up the walls so it doesn't collapse in on itself. A bucket on a winch hung above it can be used to draw the water. However, there are many downsides to this type of well. Firstly, the initial water at the bottom will be heavily particle-laden, e.g. muddy, so you must wait for it to fill substantially and settle before drawing water. Secondly, because of the large entrance hole, animals, birds and insects have a tendency to fall in and die, making the water unpotable. This can be solved by making a cover for the hole but dirt, leaves and other detritus still will find their way in. Also, if the water table gets too low there is a good chance that the water at the bottom will turn brackish – which means you have to fill in the well and start over in another location.

A better, and more modern, option is to have a well drilled and a thin steel pipe sunk into the ground. This is then capped with a pump, drastically limiting any external contamination. The water can still become brackish during a drought, however.

Some wells are fitted with electric pumps to make connecting to taps and boilers within the home easier but this is a costly solution – unless you utilize an alternative energy source such as solar power. For the traditionalist, the best method is the hand pump. It means more work each day but it won't cost you anything.

Traditionally, suitable locations for wells are found using dowsing rods. It's easy and fun to make your own.; Simply get two copper welding rods approximately 50cms in length, bend the first 10cms into a right angle and hold one in each fist loosely so that the long part can swing freely over the top of your first finger. Walk around your garden picturing water in your mind. When the rods cross in front of you and you feel a pull downwards, dig.

Another alternative to springs and wells is a stream. Remember that even if water looks clean it generally isn't – many microbes, bacteria and parasites are microscopic and, unless you fancy salmonella, typhoid, cholera, tapeworm or just gastroenteritis, don't drink water straight from the source. You need to purify it first. There are entire survival manuals dedicated to building your own home-made filtration kit, or at what temperature water should be pasteurized and for how long but I would recommend, if you're going to use a stream for your long term water source, to invest in a high-end water filtration system. At the minimum, you'll need one which prevents ALL bacteria down to one micron and, if you've got the money, go for one which will also prevent viruses. I use the Sawyer system as it is popular with UN relief agencies throughout the world and is capable of filtering millions of gallons from any water source (including swimming pools) using a simple bucket-to-bucket technique.

If you find yourself in a completely dire situation then:

1. Clean and purify a water container

2. Filter your water using a tight gauze such as a stocking, then leave the water to settle so that sediments drop to the bottom

3. Filter settled water again using multiple layers of charcoal and sand, then leave to settle

4. Add 2 drops of clear, unscented chlorine bleach for every litre. Leave to settle

5. Boil water for at least a minute, then leave to settle. Alternatively, pasteurize the water at 65 degrees centigrade for 20 minutes, then leave to settle, then shake the water to bring life and taste back into it

6. Pour cleansed water into cleansed container

7. Drink

Some may argue that the method just described is overkill but water can carry so many nasties – parasites, harmful bacteria and viruses – that it's worth making sure that it's been purified well. Always remember – clean looking water outside of a domestic pipe system probably isn't very clean.

If there's one thing guaranteed to make you very ill, even kill you, in a SITX, then it's drinking unpurified water.

Currency

"*I think money is due for some sort of collapse. People are going to realize that money has a half-life, like radioactive elements.*"

—Doug Coupland

"*I believe that thrift is essential to well-ordered living.*"

—John D. Rockefeller

Keep hold of your credit card and realize that if you spend more money than you actually possess then whatever you own is in fact legally owned by someone else, e.g. a bank, until you pay off your debt.

The No.1 aim of all preppers should be in becoming self-sufficient. Going into debt with faceless corporate bankers kind of defeats that aim, and is primarily why most countries are sinking fast.

It's like when people drive around in big cars bought on HP or loan so that they can show others how rich they are. Until they've paid off every last penny, they're merely borrowing it at a high monthly cost.

I'd rather be poor and standing on my own two feet than materialistically overburdened and owned by banks. It's not exactly good practice for a SHTF scenario.

Rather than buy stuff, learn to make your own. Ultimately, you're prepping for you and your family and not to show others what you've got. If you can't afford something then you've got several legal options:

- save up and pay cash
- find a cheaper option
- make your own
- wait until the price drops
- buy small and slowly
- buy second hand

Don't fall into the trap that banks and advertising agencies and superstores set for you. There are loads of things I'd love to buy, and banks would be more than happy to give me the funds for them (at a price) but instead I either have to shrug my shoulders and forget, or find alternative means.

An example would be Internet shopping - the entire system is set up to capture impulse purchases. In the old days of E-commerce, studies were done which showed that if a customer had to do more than seven click-throughs to get to the check-out then they'd usually reconsider and cancel. Try this in real life. If there's anything you want to buy, write it down on a piece of paper, look up reviews, etc. but don't buy it. Come back in a month and look at your piece of paper again. Do you really need it? Chances are that you don't and you'll have saved that money (or spent it on something more necessary).

> *"When the last tree is cut, the last fish is caught, and the last river is polluted; when to breathe the air is sickening, you will realize, too late, that wealth is not in bank accounts and that you can't eat money."*

—Alanis Obomsawin

At present, there is a huge drive to make this a cashless society. If this continues we will only be able to make electronic transactions. With fears over economic collapse, many have begun investing in precious metals, although this should have been done several years ago before they had a massive rise in price. Now they have dropped significantly again, especially gold. While they most likely will rise again in the future, it is really wise to invest in such?

First of all, to really profit from precious metals you'll need a fair weight of them. Secondly, in a SHTF scenario, just how easily transferable would they be when trying to buy food or goods? Value is dictated by the buyer's willingness to pay and the scarcity of the product – who is to say what the price of an egg will be when there is only one chicken left standing?

Unless you have a large amount of money sitting idle, and know what you're doing, buying precious metals might not be the way to go. If you do decide to go that route then make sure you buy physical gold or silver or platinum, e.g. coins or bullion, and never paper, e.g. shares or stocks. The world currently has approximately 750 tonnes of gold bullion, yet on paper this been leveraged to fantastic amounts which simply don't exist. The paper you invest in might be worth nothing but paper.

For the true self-reliant prepper, look into gold panning. Equip yourself with a decent set of pans and a sluice and go find your own gold. There are a multitude of websites, forums and online videos which can teach you the basics. Gold panning is a natural extension of prepping and homesteading as it gets you out into the countryside and you're doing something by yourself which can benefit your family. Turn the trip into a picnic and get the whole family involved, perhaps do a spot of fishing, foraging or crayfish potting while you're there...

Forget diamonds, regardless of what the salesman tries to tell you about them being the ultimate heirloom or investment. Global diamond prices are fixed by a certain Belgian company, and there are in fact so many diamonds in existence that in reality they're virtually worthless. Most diamonds are used in industry rather than for jewellery. And then there are the new synthetic diamonds which are identical to the natural ones, so you might not even be buying what you expected.

If you're on a small budget then forget getting rich post-apocalypse with shiny things, unless you live in a country where ammunition may be legally stored as this will rise exponentially in value. Think about things you would miss personally, or your friends and family, and then stock up on those plus keep a surplus for barter and trade. Toilet paper, tobacco, good alcohol such as whiskey, sweets, chocolate, pens and pencils, women's sanitary products, perfume, socks and underwear, first aid kits, medicine and antibiotics, painkillers, spectacles, fuel, batteries, water purification tablets, powdered drinks, tea, coffee, sugar, salt, various spices and hot sauces, boot laces...

Use your imagination.

Survivors of a cataclysm will learn to reuse what they have, and to repair, but life and especially food will quickly become bland. In return for their services you can supply them with little luxuries. Wandering, masterless samurai, *ronin*, often received only a few bowls of rice and a bed per day for their services.

Just don't flaunt what you've got or someone will try to take it off you.

To bring this concept into the present world and provide an excellent Grey Man cover, open a small shop. You'll make money, have goods in store for when needed, and you'll be able to rotate stock so that it doesn't go bad.

Remember, it may all come down to bartering so brush up on your haggling skills...

Burn Out

"Take rest; a field that has rested gives a bountiful crop"

—Ovid

The day slipped into evening without me noticing. It wasn't until pink streaks scored the pale pastel blue of the sky visible between the tips of the conifers through the window of my studio that I realized time had passed me by. The sun was almost gone and already the mice were busying themselves in the attic above, their scratching and pitter-patter running an ambient setting after dusk.

The sheer beauty of the sunset captivated me and I felt like a deer or rabbit caught in headlamps. Inside, I felt pain and sorrow that such a moment couldn't be held onto, that it was but a brief passing image of natural beauty which would, in a couple of more minutes, disappear forever. Part of me wanted to go find the camera, to waste what little time there was left attempting to capture the scene, knowing full well that all previous attempts at capturing sunsets had turned out to be a disappointment. Part of me wanted to look away, to stop torturing myself with the ephemeral. However, the part of me which tries to understand the fleeting nature of the moment decided to just watch and enjoy it while it lasted. Hopefully, there would be another the next day, or perhaps the day after.

There comes a point in every prepper's journey when it all becomes too much. Prepping, like any activity, is healthy only when it doesn't begin to interfere negatively with your normal life. However, prepping, by its very nature, obviously does interfere quite severely with what most people would call a normal life, so how can you find a balance? How can you know when you're going too far and it's time for a break?

There are a few common behavioural and personality issues which can mistakenly find a new home in prepping and, if you suffer from any of these, then you need to analyse yourself and work out how to curb them. Probably the three most common ones, bizarrely enough, are hoarding, shopaholism and OCD, obsessive compulsive disorder.

Prepping, again by its very nature, generally requires the storing of goods – food stuffs, equipment and so on. This, in and of itself, is a positive action as it is preparation for the well-being of yourself and your family in the future. When a prepper stops throwing things away because everything might have a use, old newspapers by the bundle or food long past its sell-by-date, then this is no longer prepping. A certain amount of hygiene must be maintained, along with a navigable home. If you discover that you have reached such a point, or others are telling you that you have, where acquiring or storing things has begun to get in the way of your normal life, then ask a friend to help you clear the mess. Ask a close friend and then trust their decision on what should stay and what really needs to go. Be honest with yourself.

If you know you're a shopaholic then set yourself a definite budget for your preps – weekly, monthly etc. – and stick to it. The urge to go out and completely outfit your home, BOL, BOB, etc. can be very overwhelming but control yourself. One of the principle aims of self-reliance is to get yourself out of debt, not go deeper into it.

Shopaholism and OCD often join together when it comes to perfecting kit. Having the ultimate ECD or GHB is, to some, an unattainable Grail and instead becomes a continuous cycle of buying new equipment to replace old, quickly feeling unsatisfied with it due to poor online reviews or a new release or even just personal dissatisfaction after use, and then buying even newer. When contemplating your initial attempts at putting together kit, for whatever purpose, don't allow similar kits of veteran preppers to make you want to throw away your budget and go on a spending spree.

I'll be honest, sometimes it's depressing seeing what others have amassed. Prepping, like any other activity, does have a wide range of equipment ranging from the cheap and not so cheerful, right up to the Gucci level, with prices to match. Work your way up to it, if you ever really need to, which in all honesty you don't, by experiencing and using the basics and understanding what you personally need. Listen to others' recommendations but don't ruin yourself just to get something you might not even personally like.

The other issue which can have an effect on the prepper is burn-out. This can happen when someone has become so pre-occupied with stocking up or trying to learn too many new skills that it begins taking a toll on their personal lives. It also happens when people fixate on what they can't realistically afford but believe without which they can't progress any further; for example, thinking that without having total solar power and a well and a fully kitted out Bug Out Vehicle then they're basically wasting their time, yet they haven't yet got in a month's worth of food. Fretting overly about possible future scenarios is also to blame.

Burn-out can affect anyone and the best way to prevent it is to continue to do your normal, everyday activities. When you meet with friends and family outside of the prepping community, then don't talk about prepping. This is also good Grey Man OPSEC, or operational security.

If you get invited to a party then go to it. I've known preppers cancel holidays abroad because they were worried that something might happen while they were away and they wouldn't be in reach of their equipment! Ignoring their lack of foresight in packing a modified EDC and GHB, they're missing out on living now by fixating on the possible future.

Carpe diem! Seize the day!

Sometimes it may be necessary to take a step back from your prepping for a while – possibly because of family issues, or because of work commitments, or because you need time to re-evaluate your life. Don't worry about this. Use the time for what you need to do; your preps will be waiting for you when you return. You may even bring fresh new ideas or want to change what you've already done. Priests sometimes go on sabbatical when their faith is in doubt or when they're tired from their daily chores – there's no reason you can't do the same.

Keep prepping positive, healthy and enjoyable. Prepare for the future but live life now.

Tao of Prepping

Technology

The storm began long before it arrived. The distant, almost continuous rumble of thunder, the leaves rustling in the trees and the upper branches swaying, especially the willows. The electric bulbs hanging in lamps from the ceiling weakened and flickered.

Then came the first crack of lightning. The thunder shook the house. The dog barked in panic and the swing bench somersaulted down the garden. Another immense crack of lightning and the lights went out. Dust and leaves and other wind-borne matter slammed into the windows.

I reached into my pocket, withdrew a cigarette lighter and proceeded to light the various candles dotted about the place. I lit the fire in the hearth and kept my head torch handy. I sat down on the couch and my dog curled up, growling beside me. The storm raged on but I had warmth, shelter, light, water and a faithful companion with me. The sheer magnitude of the storm more than compensated for the lack of electricity. It was both stimulating and frightening and I was at the heart of it – far better than passively watching some action or thriller shown on TV.

By now, you're probably expecting that I'll suggest some sort of Luddite rebellion, a complete rejection of all modern technology and that I'll recommend a return to some quasi-Amish existence. You'd be wrong.

We're not what we were, hundreds or thousands of years ago. We cannot even perceive the world in the way our ancestors did, when life expectancy was about 30 and plagues, wars, banditry, slavery and servitude were part and parcel of normal life. When it was normal to lose half of your children either in childbirth or during infancy from illnesses we don't even worry about today. When even the shortest distance between two locations required a dangerous expedition but most people rarely left the place where they were born. When there was no education, except for a trade which, once entered, would be what you did for life and which would most likely give you your surname: Peter the Butcher, Joan the Slopper...

When there was no social climbing, except in battle, from which most would return disfigured and lacking various limbs, which would mean no work, which would mean a slow death from starvation. When there was virtually no social net for the orphan, for the poor, for the old, for the handicapped; where worth was based on function and physical capability.

In many ways we live in idyllic times where we have the freedom to even conceive of rejecting it all and adopting a faux pastoral lifestyle, much like French aristocrats liked to do in the 17th and 18th centuries.

We discuss these ideas over the Internet with other similarly lucky people, or we chat about them on touch-screen mobile phones. We drive to RVs, or group camps, in four wheel drive, air conditioned, horseless carriages, or perhaps come by train or bus. Some of us even fly in giant metal birds.

We listen to radios for the news and weather forecasts, we watch how-to and review videos on the monitor connected to our computer or laptop, or even on a Tablet while lying in a bath filled with hot water which has been treated, heated and pumped indoors.

When we're ill we automatically expect that a medical professional will cure us quickly with a medicine, or painlessly with an operation. If we think ourselves ugly we can have our faces and bodies physically altered to make us more attractive so that we don't have to bear such a deformity for the whole of our lives.

We buy equipment cheaply and easily, equipment which would have been pure fantasy, if it were even conceived of, but a hundred years ago. We no longer buy, or make, one thing for life, nor do we have to take care of it as we know we can always replace it. We buy, sell and move house at whim – we're not tied to the land.

There is no going back. We just can't. Even after a world-changing cataclysm there would still be remnants of our civilization left for us to use. It may need to be looked after more, and repaired often as we might lose the ability to reproduce it en masse, but this is where welders and electricians and mechanics would come into force. We would still need to rely on even the most basic of technology in order to survive.

We're no longer hardy. Survival of the fittest went out the window long ago. We're lazy, we're fat, our bodies are utterly dependent on chemicals and sugars. We see walking as an organized sporting activity rather than the primary means of getting from A to B. We use equipment daily which 99% of us have no real idea how it is made or how it works – a true peasant basically makes everything they own due to the necessity of poverty, not through choice.

As such, we must become hybrids. Without squandering the few remaining resources that this planet has left to offer, we should be focusing on creating reusable, long-lasting technology. Rather than introducing new gizmos every 6 months and tossing away the old, we should be building updatable ones which require only the tiniest of adjustments to improve them. This would come from re-introducing a sense of pride in what we do and what we make, rather than making the fastest possible profit and basically creating disposable junk.

As preppers, it is important that we intimately know all the equipment we intend to rely on should the lights go out, how to repair it and, ideally, how to reproduce it. Don't for a moment imagine it will be easy going from a technologically dependent lifestyle to one without. In order to slowly acclimatize you should have periods now where you deliberately switch off the power and see how you fare. It will teach you and your family a lot about what you never thought you'd miss, and what you never imagined you'd need.

It is paradoxical that while we shouldn't be dependent on technology it would be silly to reject it. There are various items of equipment which technology has updated to the point where it can be run via solar power or clockwork, meaning no more batteries or electricity – radios, torches and lanterns, even showers. This is how we should be embracing and utilizing technology.

Clockwork and/or solar-powered necessities

Many preppers buy the latest kit purely for use post-SHTF, when they know that they'll need the best the modern world can produce in order to survive in the world following. While this is a good idea in theory, it puts them in far more precarious a position than those preppers who know how to make and repair their own equipment from scrap found lying around. Having the knowledge to make a knife, grow veg, build or repair a house or vehicle, assemble and use a short wave radio, install a well and plumbing, make and repair clothing, raise bees and make honey and candles, cure basic ailments using herbs and modern first aid techniques, understand modern scientific and medical theories concerning water purification, cooking, bacteria, hygiene and so on, this is what all preppers should be doing to bridge the gap between the technological and the primitive.

And the best time to learn and practice is now, while the lights are still on.

Winter

"Love keeps the cold out better than a cloak."

—Henry Wadsworth Longfellow

Most people think of winter survival in terms of digging snow holes or building igloos in an Arctic wasteland. After all, that's what most survival guides suggest. But most of us won't ever come into contact with such bleak locations – not unless we're unlucky enough to crash during a transatlantic flight. However, the world's weather patterns are changing – we're getting extreme heat and drought followed by torrential rain and perpetual flooding, all rounded off by Siberian sub-zero winters and heavy snow fall. Winter 2011-12 saw European seas freezing over and Winter, 2012-13 lasted until mid-April. If there was ever a time to start prepping for the realities of a harsh winter, then it would be now.

Winter doesn't usually properly kick in here until January, when local temperatures last year plunged to below minus 30 degrees Centigrade and hard icy snow carpeted the landscape for several months.

Any decent survival instructor will tell you that in order to survive you'll need shelter, water, food and warmth. Remove any one of those and I guarantee it will become your sole obsession until you manage to sort it out.

Winter's a long and serious affair over here in Eastern Slovakia and people prepare well for it. When I see the chaos brought on by a couple of days of snow in the UK, it makes me wonder why people don't just make a few preparations prior and they'd ride it out with relative ease. It's worthwhile putting a little effort into making sure you and your family are ready just in case. Don't wait for the rescue services to come and dig you out – they'll be busy trying to help those who really need their aid, such as the live-alone elderly.

Start off by making your car winter-ready. Invest in a set of snow tyres. In many parts of Europe these are a legal requirement in winter and they can save your life. With a little practice, they'll enable you to drive on snow and ice with ease. Keep a snow shovel and a couple of sheets of cardboard (or a bag of gravel) in the boot – these will enable you to get a grip if you end up in a drift. Rubber floor mats just don't compare.

Use antifreeze. Keep a change of warm clothing, a first aid kit and a torch in the car. Throw in a couple of bottles of juice and some chocolate bars with them, maybe even a space blanket, and if you do find yourself marooned overnight in a blizzard there's a good chance you won't be found like an icicle the next day.

At home, stock up on a week's worth of easily cookable food (tins, rice, pasta, etc. not microwavable). Rotate it (use old and buy new) so it doesn't go off. Keep it tucked away somewhere with a cool temperature for when you need it. Keep a calor gas stove (and full tank) somewhere handy, and only switch it on when the electricity or gas mains go off. A wind-up radio will keep you both informed and entertained – they don't cost a lot and can be a godsend when you're sitting there shivering in candlelight.

Buy a sleeping bag for each member of your family, preferably ones with hood attached, so you can crawl into them under your duvets to keep cosy and warm; choose bags which are at least 3 season.

Get a couple of large jerry cans (20 litres or so) for storing water – make sure ONLY water is kept in them. Keep them somewhere that won't freeze and fill them two-thirds full just in case ice starts to form. You'll also need an alternative means of cooking to your gas stove or electric hob – a butane camping stove is a good option but remember that it is a fire hazard and will release toxic fumes so should only be used in a ventilated environment. Make sure you have a good set of winter clothes, gloves, scarves, hats and snow boots for all the family – remember to change them and dry them out when they get wet. Don't sit in wet clothes.

Keep an eye out for hypothermia – if a family member begins acting sleepy, sluggish or lethargic (at least more than usual...), warm them up. Snuggling up next to someone and sharing body heat isn't just fun, it's life-saving. Develop a sense of community – look out for your neighbours. If you know someone old or infirm then make sure they're okay, and don't just take a polite dismissal. Invite them over to share a meal or even just a chat; help dig out their driveway and let them know that there's someone out there for them if they need it.

Prepping isn't just for hardcore survivalists, it means thinking ahead and making sure that if something dire should happen then you won't be left with your pants hanging around your ankles and in a position where you need to beg the rescue services to come dig you out.

As the scouts say: *Be prepared.*

Don't be a burden, be an asset.

© National Geographic Channels/Bullseye TV

Ranged Weapons

"Whether the Kinges subjectes, not lame nor having no lawfull impediment, and beinge within the age of XI (11) yeares, excepte Spiritual men, Justices etc. and Barons of the Exchequer, use shoting on longe bowes, and have bowe continually in his house, to use himself and that fathers and governours of chyldren teach them to shote, and that bowes and arrowes be bought for chyldren under XVII (17) and above VII (7) yere, by him that has such a chylde in his house, and the Maister maye stoppe it againe of his wages, and after that age he to provideb them himselfe: and who that is founde in defaute, in not having bowes and arrowes by the space of a moneth, to forfayte xiid (12p)...

...And that buttes be made, in everie citie, towne and place accordinge to the law of auncient time used, and the inhabitantes and dwellers in everye of them to exercise themselfe with longe bowes in shotinge at the same, and elles wher on holy daies and other times conveniente."

—King Henry VIII, Statute ANNO 6. H8.
Cap:2. (1515)

When it comes to hunting and defending your home or family then unless you're a bonafide ninja you're going to want to do both at a distance. In hunting terms, the further away you can successfully take down your quarry, the more likely you are to actually take it down – animals have keen ears and sense of smell. One foot wrong or if the wind changes, your quarry will bolt before you've closed in. In terms of defence, the more things you can fling at a potential attacker before *they* close in, the more chance you have of incapacitating them and therefore removing them as a viable threat.

The British Government, in its infinite wisdom, decided to disarm the general populace (unless you're a violent criminal, then this doesn't affect you) and take away basically everything that goes *bang*. This means that, unlike our American cousins, the average British citizen's only recourse during an armed attack is to call **999** and hope for the best. After all, shooting an armed home-invader bent on raping and killing your family would violate his human rights.

But all is not lost. We didn't win Agincourt with automatic rifles, nor Crecy with shotguns. We do have other options. The Americans would probably laugh but only until they have personally experienced the penetration and shock damage of a bolt fired from a 150 lb crossbow. While it isn't a .357 Magnum, the person or animal on the receiving end is unlikely to quibble about such details.

Bows

There are several types of bow available. Forget the traditional English Longbow unless you're experienced at archery and have the muscles to use one. Also, they require a lot of TLC. And they're huge. And, generally, very expensive.

Compound bows usually have enough foot poundage to bring down most large game, are more compact than other types of bow, and are quite easy to use, but unless you're mechanically minded and have both the spare parts and tools to fix them when the cam, wheel, cable or string break, best to leave them to more civilized times.

Recurves are your best bet. A good recurve bow (you'll need at least 50lb draw weight) armed with broadhead arrows will keep your larder stocked and your home free from most undesirables. Rather than get a natural bow (made from wood, sinew, bone, or other laminates), get yourself one made from modern materials, along with several spare strings. Natural bows do strange things depending on the weather as the wood they're made from expands, contracts and sometimes even explodes – fibreglass bows are far more resilient. A 3-piece take-down recurve bow should see you right. Just make sure you start practising now and don't leave it until you actually need the bow in a survival situation. They're not as easy to use as Hollywood makes out.

Crossbows

Unlike bows, which take years to really get to grips with, crossbows are basically point-and-shoot weapons. If you're capable of drawing the string back and cocking the beast (with larger crossbows you'll need pulleys and cranks to help you), then you're capable of shooting one. A crossbow is the closest thing the average British citizen can get to a firearm and, after practice, is just as useful. However, they're generally quite bulky, are difficult to load and have way too many parts which could potentially break. If you fancy yourself as a mechanic and know how to metalwork then you could make your own.

Crossbows come in two main types – the recurve and the compound. As with bows, the extreme complexity of the compound style makes them redundant for a survival situation, so go with the recurve (it has only one string). And buy as many spare parts, bolts and strings as you can now.   Post-apocalyptic mail order might drag…

In terms of size, crossbows generally come in a T-shaped rifle form or as a T-shaped pistol. If you're planning on using your crossbow for home defence or in a tight space then go with the pistol bow. They usually come in either 50lb or 80lb draw weights and modern versions have a self-cocking arm which will make life much easier for you. If you can, get the 80lb one with suitable bolts and it'll stop most things which try to get through your door at close range. If you're planning on hunting game then go for as large a draw weight as possible in the rifle format, get yourself a good spot or telescopic sight and, of course, some decent bolts.

Bows and crossbows often come with target bolts and arrows made from fibreglass and with aluminium tips. Aim for aluminium bolts (or arrows), with steel tips – broadheads for game, bodkins for armour.

If you're planning on Bugging-In then a decent crossbow should be No.1 on your priority list.

Catapults

I'm not joking. Not only are they capable of firing a spherical missile a great distance but they're also capable of taking down both game and people. Modern catapults are ergonomically shaped, can have arm support rests and stabilizers, and, best of all, can fire any small stone, nut, marble, conker, etc you can find so you'll never run out of ammo. I really recommend keeping one for backup at least.

There are two major customizations I'd recommend to anyone getting a catapult – change the store-provided elastic with some heavy duty fitness stuff (the professionals all use Theraband) and also adapt it (or, at least a second one) into a sling bow. This means you can fire an arrow from your catapult and it turns a schoolboy's toy into a lethal, silent, portable weapon.

One other thing I'd really suggest is that you start practising now with your catapult as you don't want to wait until you're weak from starvation to discover that the stone doesn't fly how you thought.

Airguns

Ignoring the sniggers from across the pond as they cradle their semi-automatics, airguns do have a very productive place in the survivalist's ambient. While pretty useless for defence (unless you go over the 12 ft lb legal limit and then you're breaking the law) – excluding the annoyance value ("Ow! Stop bloody shooting me! Ow!") or it being used as a club – an airgun is far more likely to put meat on your table than any other ranged weapon legally available to the common peasantry in the UK.

There are two main sizes of round (.22 and .177) and two main types (pistol and rifle). As any poacher will tell you, the rule is .177 for birds and .22 for rabbits and other similar sized varmints. At a push you'd probably take down a fox with a head-shot with a steel sabot .22. The .22 lead pellet is heavier and adds shock value which might stun rather than kill but if you get to the animal quickly enough you can finish it off with a neck wrench. Birds, and especially waterfowl, on the other hand, have tightly packed feathers which can sometimes repel the slower, heavier, .22, so a pointy .177 is more useful. Birds depend heavily on balance for flying and a pellet in the ribs or in the wing will usually ground them, meaning you can then rush in for a neck wrench.

If you're getting an air rifle (as with everything else) get a good one. It's worth spending the money to ensure that you don't end up with a bent or loose fitting barrel. Similarly, be careful with it as barrels bend (and it will no longer seal properly) when dropped and then you'll end up with a traditional funfair job – where it hits is anyone's guess.

Forget about airpistols. They're useless for all intents and purposes, at least at the levels you can legally buy. Instead, a 50lb pistol-bow will easily take down a pheasant or rabbit from 10 yards and is also pretty damned intimidating.

Spears, boomerangs, atlatl, slings, shuriken etc.

While it would be an adrenaline rush to scream "I'm gonna get Paleolithic on you!", the sheer amount of practice required to use any of these proficiently rules them out for the average 9 to 5er. Perhaps after Armageddon when you have a bit more time on your hands you can make your own...

So why do we prep?

"For brick and mortar breed filth and crime,
With a pulse of evil that throbs and beats;
And men are whithered before their prime
By the curse paved in with the lanes and streets.

And lungs are poisoned and shoulders bowed,
In the smothering reek of mill and mine;
And death stalks in on the struggling crowd—
But he shuns the shadow of the oak and pine"

—George W. Sears Nessmuk, Woodcraft and
Camping

Just a few decades ago, still in living memory, everyone practised self-reliance. There was no NHS, no Welfare benefits, and no free housing. Mortgages and bank loans were only for the rich.

Health and safety came from parental wisdom and learned experience. True, life was harder but it was also more real.

And then it all changed.

Slowly we began relinquishing our personal opinions, freedom and choice and placed them in the hands of others- health organisations, governmental bodies, planning councils; in umbrella terms the "Nanny State".

> *"Those who would give up essential liberty to purchase a little temporary safety deserve neither liberty nor safety"*
>
> —Benjamin Frankiln

We relinquished liberty for safety and reality for fantasy. We became ensnared in the nets of major corporations - pharmaceutical, agricultural, financial, media, automotive, technological, etc. We began comparing our boring, meagre existence with what was shown to us continuously on TV and in adverts and, as luck would have it, we were offered financial loans in order to pay for a drastic life change.

In the space of 100 years we have gone from requiring an immense unskilled labour population for factories to requiring a handful of multi-skilled technology experts. Yet, instead of slowly reducing this unemployable population, the Nanny State encouraged its growth by feeding and housing it and its progeny, and bizarrely, importing more from all quarters of the Earth.

"The welfare state is collapsing all around us. There are people that realize that we can't go on this way, but I'm not sure how many people realize how close we are to the collapse of the U.S. financial system".

—Rush Limbaugh

We can no longer afford to live in the housing we built our fantasies on, nor can we afford to pay the debts that we were encouraged to take on because every industry has been sold or shipped overseas, leaving little required workforce.

We have handed over our rights as parents to anonymous social workers and government think tanks who decide who gets to keep their child and who not; the same policy makers who thought banning smacking would be a good idea even when it resulted in hundreds of thousands of delinquent youths whose only expectancy in life is that the State will keep them and that no one will ever punish them.

We have watched as the concept of 'family' has been erased from our social consciousness over the last 40 years even though family is the centre of all civilized, and self-reliant, life. Where old people are to be kept in special homes and fed by the State, where divorce is normal, and single parent teenage families are a good example for the children they are raising. By removing the family we have become isolated, alone and easily managed.

We have been stripped of the right to even carry a knife, never mind anything with a barrel. We can no longer travel freely on open spaces unless we stick to a signposted path; nor are we allowed to sleep outside of our heavily taxed and mortgaged homes unless we pay for the privilege and share a wash-block.

We have stopped learning trades and instead we're conditioned to be *officeniks,* to spend the rest of our lives sitting in cubicles and staring at a monitor. Our free time involves sitting in front of a box watching other people singing or dancing or redecorating their homes and being ridiculed.

> *"We may get to the point where the only way of saving the world will be for industrial civilization to collapse."*

—Maurice Strong

We feed our children on poisonous corporate-grown food, bought in flashy carcinogenic plastic packaging from corporate owned mega-stores, which we cook in a nuclear box.

We no longer speak face-to-face, instead we use little brain-cancer inducing boxes into which we speak or tap messages, all of which are recorded and stored in huge memory banks by various parties, and which constantly give our GPS position away.

Our youth die in corporate-sponsored wars fighting for oil fields and opium crops and find themselves lost when they come home as they're an unmentionable aspect of corporate greed which doesn't fit into polite society.

Our ancient countryside traditions have been outlawed by wealthy suburbanites, and our farms either lie fallow or produce poisonous genetically modified crops which eradicate the local flora and fauna.

Our heads are unrelentingly filled with fear from the media - the old fear the young, the whites fear immigrants, and we all fear the economy and even the weather.

> *A WOLF, meeting a big well-fed Mastiff with a wooden collar about his neck asked him who it was that fed him so well and yet compelled him to drag that heavy log about wherever he went. "The master," he replied. Then said the Wolf: "May no friend of mine ever be in such a plight; for the weight of this chain is enough to spoil the appetite."*

—Aesop

So why do we prep?

Because we know that we, as individuals, have no affect on the *status quo*. We're not powerful enough to stand up to corporations or corrupt bureaucrats, yet each of us is sickened that our once beautiful land has, to all effects, been locked and barred from us. We miss nature and feeling at one with the land. We miss the adrenaline and sense of pride at being able to provide our families with food, clothing and shelter from our own toil and without the help of banks or infinite legislation. We miss facing the elements and the wild and carving our own place in it.

But it goes much deeper than that, much, much deeper, and it begins with a simple premise. Each of us was born on Planet Earth. Each of us has a potential lifespan of 70 years, and then we die. Each and every one of us. Not one of us is exempt. A few specimens of humanity live to 100; many of us die much earlier. But we all die. We all have a finite time in which to live.

But there's the rub... We don't live. We exist, we avoid, we hunker down and hope that life misses us out. We try not to tempt fate. Life terrifies us, independent thought gives us nightmares...

Until we deliberately decide to do otherwise and to take our own lives in our hands and start on the path to self-reliance.

So we hope, secretly and unconsciously pray, that some *deus ex machina* steps in and stops it all for us. That some major catastrophe brings it all to a halt so that we may once again stand on our own two feet. We prep because we don't want to end up like the millions who rely utterly on the Nanny State. We prep so that, with a bit of luck and a global calamity, we may once again live as free men and women, from the sweat of our own brows and under decent moral laws and rights.

Because without that TEOTWAWKI event we're powerless and trapped within a system which was designed by and for a completely different type of person, a tiny powerful minority.

> *"To compel a man to furnish contributions of money for the propagation of opinions which he disbelieves and abhors is sinful and tyrannical."*
>
> —Thomas Jefferson

One thing that always seems to go unsaid or overlooked is that every single person born on this planet has as much right as the next. No single person, or corporate entity, has the right to 'privatize' water or ban the growing of foodstuffs, or enforce payment from another merely to live - that's called extortion.

So we prep and hope because we're not strong enough to do otherwise...

And, perhaps, because something wicked this way comes....

Spera optimum sed

Praepara ad pessimum

The Yeoman's Creed

I was born a free individual, a native of Planet Earth.

As an intelligent person I have the right to make my own decisions concerning myself and my children. So long as I harm no other, unless in self-defence, or steal from them or damage their property, I have the right to live my short life on Earth as I choose without fear of others ordering me or forcing me to do otherwise.

I have the right to choose which plants to grow and consume. I have the right to choose which livestock I shall raise. I have the right to cultivate my own property in order to provide food and sustenance for myself and my family. I have the right to drill a well to provide water for my family.

I have the right to seek out sustainable alternatives for fuel and energy so that neither I, nor my family, become indebted to companies and corporations, nor be a burden on dwindling resources.

I have the right to build whatever property I choose on my own private land, and to make whatever modifications I like to it, otherwise it is not private land. I do not need to seek another's permission to do this.

I have the right to protect myself and my family from harm in the manner that best befits the situation; any person who wishes to harm myself, my family, or my property has relinquished their right to civilized conduct and must face the consequences of their actions.

I have the right to decide which individual or group of individuals decide the fate of myself and my family. I have the right to reject the commands of those I deem irrelevant to my life or my family's lives. This is called freedom of choice and any enforcement otherwise is merely extortion, torture, kidnapping, blackmail, a protection racket or tyranny and as such is an illegal act under Common Law.

I have the right to choose what education my family will receive without fear of being imprisoned illegally or having my children stolen from me. I agree that all children need to learn how to read, write and perform arithmetic calculations but any subject beyond that is optional and must not be enforced.

I have the right to decide which medicine and medical treatment both I and my family will receive and have the right to refuse any I deem harmful or unnecessary.

I have the right to choose my own religious and sexual persuasion.

I was born a free individual, I will live as a free individual, and I shall die a free individual.

I am a Yeoman.

Thus begins the Tao of Prepping....

Tao of Prepping

Glossary

BI	Bugging In. Turning your house into a fort and staying put
Bivvy	Short for bivouac, the most basic form of shelter
BO	Leaving home and heading to the wilderness
BOB	Bug Out Bag. The container for carrying all the things you'll need to survive away from home for a long period of time, often designated by time lengths such as 24 hours, 72 hours, or INCH
BOL	Bug Out Location. The place you head to to ride out the storm

BOV | Bug Out Vehicle. The vehicle you use to escape a disaster situation, often a 4x4 or a motorbike

Bushcrafter | Someone who uses primitive and traditional technology and techniques in a natural setting, e.g. a forest

EDC | Every Day Carry. Everything you carry about your person, or in your bag, pockets or purse, when going about your daily life

FAK | First Aid Kit

GHB | Get Home Bag. The container for carrying enough equipment to get you safely back home if you're at work or away when disaster strikes

Homesteader | Someone who has turned their home and land into a self-sufficient farm, or who is in the process of doing so

INCH | I'm Not Coming Home. When Bugging Out is intended to be permanent

OPSEC | Operational Security – Loose lips sink ships, and all that

Prepper	Someone who prepares in advance for possible
Recce	Reconnaissance —To investigate a location, person or situation before taking decisive action
SAK	Swiss Army Knife
SHTF	Shit Hits The Fan, usually following 'when the...' - this often denotes the point at which normal life ceases to exist
SITX	Situation X. When normal life comes to a crashing halt, often for an extended period, due to a catastrophe
Tacticool	a) A piece of equipment which is both tactical (SWAT or military) and cool, often specialised and expensive; b) Derogatory, a person who wears the latest tactical equipment because they want to look like they're SWAT or military
TEOTWAKI	The End Of The World As We Know It
TPTB	The Powers That Be – the elite who make all the decisions
Womble	Like the TV characters of the same name, to make use of found junk

Acknowledgements

I would like to thank the members of P2S, *Prepared To Survive* forum. We've had our ups and downs but I've learned a lot, am still learning, from you guys. You've driven me mad and you've kept me sane – I'd recommend you to anyone and everyone. Keep up the good work!

I'd also like to thank the Carpatho-Rusyn people for keeping their traditions alive so that others might still learn.

My thanks goes to Carolyn, without whom the Tao would probably not have come to light until after the SHTF.

And to Kevin and MMP – once again you saved the day.

About the Author

Edward O'Toole was born in the English city of Chester. He studied at Isaac Newton's old school, the King's School, Grantham. Later, he read Cultural Studies at Norwich School of Art and Design and, later still, Religious Studies at Nation University.

He has travelled, and lived, in many different countries, but has called Slovakia "home" for the last 15 years. He lives with his wife, three children and a dog.

Edward's main interests are writing, art, traditional living skills, and the unknown. Every book he writes is a personal progression.

He splits his time between living in the modern world and in a remote Ruthenian village, not far from Andy Warhol's, where he tries to live whilst incorporating traditional and primitive skills. Out there in the bush, he is surrounded by the history and legends of the Carpathians, as well as the many beasts which roam the forests.

"I was lucky, as a child, to have gone through Cubs, Scouts and the Combined Cadet Force at school. I was raised to both respect and appreciate nature, and many of my childhood memories are of wildlife I encountered in different countries – mink and Golden Eagles in the Hebrides, the migration of cranes in Sweden, moose in Norway, racoons, cotton mouths and Bald Eagles in Florida, *Tsefr* and jackals in Israel...

For a couple of years, when I was very young, my parents had a house in Yorkshire where they tried to live self-sufficiently, like in the series *"The Good Life"*. I think this affected me deeply and positively. As a young teen I would sleep in the woods alone, under the stars, and catch rabbits to eat.

I travelled quite a lot as a young adult and tried city living in Norwich, England, as a student, and then in Zurich, Switzerland, but it wasn't for me. When I arrived in Slovakia I thought I'd only be staying for a few months and then I'd move on but I fell in love with the wild beauty of the place. After living in a flat for a year or so I decided to buy an old cottage in a remote village, and have since spent over a decade reconstructing it.

I arrived here with western thinking and expectations but slowly, by being surrounded by a much more rustic and simplistic style of living, I began trying to copy and learn how the other villagers did things. Many things which we take for granted in the West just weren't available, or even known about, when I first arrived so I had to adapt to a make-do or improvise mentality, just like everyone else here.

The Tao of Prepping is rooted in nature, philosophy, practicality, and thrift.

Each of my books, and each set of my paintings, is a record of my exploration into the nature of life and our purpose in it. I came to the conclusion long ago that what we are told is not how it should be, that there is a far better option if only we had the strength to stand up and say 'enough is enough'.

When I see just how few extra goods the villagers require, as they can basically make or grow everything else themselves, it reminds me of just how far we in the West have removed ourselves from our own responsibility and capability, and how deeply we have fallen into modern traps. People always blame money for the situation they're in but this is often a falsity; they should be blaming themselves.

Think about this for a moment: Who would you rather make the decisions for you and your family? You? Or someone you've never met? Freedom, in whatever form, is all about setting a goal and then having the willpower and determination to reach it. Just like karma, the more help you need to attain that goal, the more you owe and the less freedom you end up with."

Remember Robin Hood and for what he stood...

www.edwardotoole.com

Did you like this book?

If you enjoyed this book, you will find more interesting books at
www.mmpubs.com

Please take the time to let us know how you liked this book. Even short reviews of 2-3 sentences can be helpful and may be used in our marketing materials.

If you take the time to post a review for this book on Amazon.com, let us know when the review is posted and you will receive a free audiobook or ebook from our catalog. Simply email the link to the review once it is live on Amazon.com, your name, and your mailing address -- send the email to orders@mmpubs.com with the subject line "Book Review Posted on Amazon."

If you have questions about this book, our customer loyalty program, or our review rewards program, please contact us at info@mmpubs.com.

Sophia Bestiae: The Wisdom of the Beast

By Edward O'Toole

After almost 2000 years of indoctrination, Man now has the chance to see God is His true light. Sophia Bestiae re-examines God, His origins and His behaviour – substantiated throughout with supporting Biblical passages – and proves that far from being the hero of the Judaeo-Christian religion, He is evil incarnate. The *Sophia Bestiae* shows that Revelations 13:18 was correct in that the Time of the Beast is now, but that The Beast is in fact Mankind – the true enemy of God. Here is wisdom. Let him that hath understanding count the number of the beast: for it is the number of a man; and his number is Six hundred threescore and six. Indexed for ease of use and quick reference, the *Sophia Bestiae* is an excellent reference guide for both beginner and advanced religious studies. For anyone who has ever noticed the contradictory behaviour of God, or has ever called their Faith into doubt, then the *Sophia Bestiae* will explain why. After reading the *Sophia Bestiae* you will be in no doubt whatsoever as to the Secret Nature of God and why He is planning Armageddon.

ISBN-13:   9781591460756
Price: $19.95

Also available in Adobe PDF ebook format.

Available from Amazon.com or your nearest book retailer. Or, order direct at www.mmpubs.com

Clavis

By Edward O'Toole

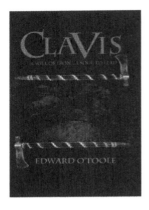

"I have watched you for several summers now, little Clavis; I have watched you more closely than you can imagine. You carry a secret that I had believed was mine alone. Many nights have I spent trying to decide your fate, and am glad I waited. Because I know you can hold your tongue I have brought you here. As of yesterday, you are a non-person as are the rest in that blasted list you heard cried. You have lost the right to a home and land; you have lost the right to work and marry. I'm trying to save your life. Here is my deal. I will save your life and you will save my family, my reputation, my Province, and the Kte. I want you to travel to Oksat."

Clavis, a young girl hunted and dispossessed, forced from her home and on a perilous journey to the barbaric lands in the far North. Cursed with a great secret and the Gift of Backsight, she must fend for herself among druids, witches, barbarians and cannibals, while avoiding those involved with a pretense to the throne.

History meets fantasy and archaeology meets magic in the harshly realistic Bronze Age *Clavis*.

ISBN-13:   9781591460350
Price: $16.95

Available from Amazon.com or your nearest book retailer. Or, order direct at www.mmpubs.com

Grimoire Bestiae

By Edward O'Toole

Sequel to the *Sophia Bestiae*, a practical working guide to the Dark Rites of the Bestian Order of Aestheteka, focusing on the Abyss, Satanic archetypes, the Luciferi and the Shadow Self. Progressive Luciferian Gnosticism. Includes: Rites of the Unpardonable Sin, Rites of Nightmares, Invocation of Satan, Rite of Necromancy, Rite of Daemons, Rite of Revenge.

ISBN-13:   9781591466666
Price: $19.95

Also available in Adobe PDF ebook format.

Available from Amazon.com or your nearest book retailer. Or, order direct at www.mmpubs.com

Carpathian Ghost Hunter: True Life Paranormal Investigations in the Land of the Blood Countess, Alzbeta Bathory

By Edward O'Toole

Thousands of years of bloody history have left the Carpathian region filled with desolate ruins and majestic castles. This is the land of Elizabeth Bathory, the Blood Countess, whose exploits have terrified children for centuries.

Edward O'Toole, the Carpathian Ghost Hunter, explores the most haunted locations this infamous region has to offer with an expansive investigation into some of Elizabeth Bathory's own castles, including Cachtica and Cicava. With over 50 black and white photographs, plus historical background details and recorded paranormal phenomenon for each location, The Carpathian Ghost Hunter presents his own findings from some of the most isolated and terrifying relics of the area.

ISBN-13:   9781591461609
Price: $16.95

Also available in Adobe PDF ebook format.

Available from Amazon.com or your nearest book retailer.
Or, order direct at www.mmpubs.com

Lightning Source UK Ltd.
Milton Keynes UK
UKOW06f2324240816

281459UK00012B/230/P